HGTV®

6 STEPS TO
DESIGN ON A DIME

MEREDITH® BOOKS
DES MOINES, IOWA

Project Manager/Writer: Amber D. Barz
Assistant Art Director: Todd Emerson Hanson
Copy Chief: Terri Fredrickson
Publishing Operations Manager: Karen Schirm
Senior Editor, Asset and Information Manager: Phillip Morgan
Edit and Design Production Coordinator: Mary Lee Gavin
Editorial Assistant: Kaye Chabot
Book Production Managers: Pam Kvitne, Marjorie J. Schenkelberg, Rick von Holdt, Mark Weaver
Contributing Copy Editor: Mark Weiford
Contributing Proofreaders: Julie Cahalan, Dan Degen, Jody Speer
Cover Photographer: Michael Garland
Contributing Photographers: Michael Garland, Tommy Miyasaki
Photostylist: Robin Tucker
Indexer: Sharon Duffy

Meredith® Books
Executive Director, Editorial: Gregory H. Kayko
Executive Director, Design: Matt Strelecki
Managing Editor: Amy Tincher-Durik
Senior Editor/Group Manager: Vicki Leigh Ingham
Senior Associate Design Director: Ken Carlson
Marketing Product Manager: Tyler Woods

Publisher and Editor in Chief: James D. Blume
Editorial Director: Linda Raglan Cunningham
Executive Director, New Business Development: Todd M. Davis
Executive Director, Sales: Ken Zagor
Director, Operations: George A. Susral
Director, Production: Douglas M. Johnston
Director, Marketing: Amy Nichols
Business Director: Jim Leonard

Vice President and General Manager: Douglas J. Guendel

Meredith Publishing Group
President: Jack Griffin
Executive Vice President: Bob Mate

Meredith Corporation
Chairman and Chief Executive Officer: William T. Kerr
President and Chief Operating Officer: Stephen M. Lacy

In Memoriam: E.T. Meredith III (1933-2003)

CONTENTS

HGTV

6 STEPS TO
DESIGN ON A DIME

What do you get when you combine one interior designer, two design coordinators, 48 hours, $1,000—and a room that needs a facelift? Great style! Exciting projects! Budget-savvy solutions!

Week after week the designers on HGTV's *Design on a Dime* transform ho-hum rooms into spaces that are stylish, functional, and just fun to be in. In this follow-up to the best-selling book *Design on a Dime: Achieve High Style on a $1,000 Budget,* you'll learn even more tips and tricks to maximize your decorating dollar without scrimping on style.

Throughout this book, *Design on a Dime* team members share their favorite decorating ideas and give you insider advice on the six design elements that guarantee decorating excellence—a well thought-out plan, inviting color, suitable furniture, coordinating fabric, beautiful artwork and accessories, and the perfect lighting. In addition to this valuable design insight, this book also includes:

• Step-by-step do-it-yourself projects—including easy-to-make furniture, artwork, and window treatments.

• 18 best-loved rooms from *Design on a Dime,* including before-and-after photos and special sidebars that cover topics from arranging furnishings to choosing color schemes.

• Charts and worksheets to help you achieve any room makeover on time and on budget.

• Innovative decorating solutions for bedrooms, baths, kitchens, dining rooms, home offices, living rooms, and outdoor spaces.

Six Simple Steps

For easy reading, this book is divided into six chapters that focus on each of the six decorating steps:

STEP **Planning for Function and Style** helps you pinpoint a design wish list, budget your project costs, and map out the entire decorating process.

STEP **Working with Color** tells you everything you need to know about choosing hues, from understanding the color wheel to finding color inspiration and ensuring your colors match.

STEP **Choosing the Perfect Furniture** explains how to identify furniture quality and how to arrange pieces to maximize comfort and achieve aesthetic balance.

STEP **Decorating with Fabric** provides fail-safe strategies for combining different fabric patterns, colors, and textures.

STEP **Accessorizing Your Room** offers clear-cut advice on how to choose and arrange artwork, accessories, and greenery.

STEP **The Right Light** shows how easily you can brighten your interiors to maximize beauty, function, and comfort.

In each chapter, photos from *Design on a Dime* episodes highlight the featured step. In addition, a tip box shows how the *Design on a Dime* teams addressed all six steps in every room makeover to create a well-rounded design. Just turn the page to begin your armchair tour!

MEET THE TEAMS

Dave Sheinkopf

For Dave Sheinkopf, New York City, where he grew up, was a breeding ground for creativity. Starting at a young age, Sheinkopf found himself in the spotlight, working on big and small screens as an actor. At age 19, he moved across the country to his new home in Los Angeles. After years of focusing his talents on television and film, he discovered a love of building and designing. Eventually set design gave way to art direction on music videos and commercials, although his passion for acting and furniture-building never subsided. His role on *Design on a Dime* feeds his creative side and has given him a great team of players to work with who are dedicated to inventing solutions for challenging decorating dilemmas.

Kristan Cunningham

Kristan Cunningham studied interior design at the University of Charleston and in 1997 introduced herself to Los Angeles and the city's cutting-edge world of design. The high-style studio where she worked gave her the opportunity to explore both the structural and technical aspects of design, providing her with an even more well-rounded design sensibility. Now as a host and designer on *Design on a Dime*, Cunningham relishes the opportunity to "get back to the basics." Viewers and readers will reap the benefits of her fresh approach to budget-conscious design.

Spencer Anderson

Spencer Anderson grew up in Houston, where he studied art and metal sculpture before moving to Tallahassee, Florida. At Florida State University, he continued to sculpt but found a new interest in designing sets and building props for his friends' movies. After graduating with a bachelor of fine arts degree, he moved to Los Angeles, where he began working as an assistant art director on small cable films. Now, as a member of the *Design on a Dime* team, he has many opportunities to make exciting pieces that don't get destroyed after the show is over! His artistic background and building talents are a perfect combination for the show's fail-safe decorating formula.

Charles Burbridge

Los Angeles native Charles Burbridge left his growing decorative painting and interiors business to join the HGTV family. Though this is his first foray into broadcast television, Burbridge has been a working actor for the past decade and is a founding member of the popular Bay Area improvisational sketch comedy troupe Big Boned Theatre. Dividing his time between his various creative pursuits has always been a challenge, but at last he has found the perfect blend of his interests and artistic abilities as a part of the *Design on a Dime* team.

Summer Baltzer

Summer Baltzer began her career more than 10 years ago, designing and decorating for community and equity theater productions in the Southern California area, while also running her own residential interior design business. She received her formal training at California State University-Northridge in the Family Environmental Sciences Department, where she studied architectural and interior design. Baltzer has many years of experience in designing interiors to suit all pocketbooks, but she particularly loves the challenge of designing a room on a dime.

Lee Snijders

Lee Snijders' former career as a Walt Disney Imagineer taught him an important lesson: As long as you have imagination, your creativity is limitless. He'll be the first to tell you he's not your stereotypical designer; his approach to design comes from his highly creative background. His inviting and sophisticated interiors range from classic midcentury modern and contemporary styles to his own unique designs. His newest career endeavor as host and designer for *Design on a Dime* encompasses both his love of entertaining and interior design. For more information about Lee Snijders, visit www.leesnijdersdesigns.com.

DESIGN THE BATH OF YOUR DREAMS

Glamorous Hollywood lights, a built-in chaise longue, and custom shelves make this bath a *Design on a Dime* all-time favorite.

FIND IT ON PAGE 42

FILL YOUR TEEN'S ROOM WITH HAPPENIN' COLOR

Mixing and matching is easy when you start with an inspiration piece.

FIND IT ON PAGE 62

GIVE YOUR BEDROOM A DREAM MAKEOVER

You can create a fresh and cohesive look by combining your existing furnishings with some new stylish and affordable finds.

FIND IT ON PAGE 84

TURN YOUR LIVING ROOM INTO A HOMEY HAVEN

Give your living room a whole new look using breezy fabrics, affordable cotton slipcovers, and secondhand finds that serve as beautiful, one-of-kind works of art.

FIND IT ON PAGE 126

TAKE YOUR KITCHEN FROM BLAND TO BEAUTIFUL

Paint, wallpaper (on the cabinets, not the walls), and the right combination of accessories can make this space look like a custom design.

FIND IT ON PAGE 154

LIGHT YOUR ROOMS TO SHOW OFF THEIR BEAUTY

(And disguise their flaws.) Make reading and other tasks easier on the eye with smart placement of fixtures.

FIND IT ON PAGE 176

STEP

1

PLANNING
FOR FUNCTION
AND STYLE

Whatever your passion—such as collecting cookbooks or pottery—a smart plan will turn a one-size-fits-all room into a tailor-made space.

When creating a budget for any room redo, keep details—such as artwork—in mind. See page 21 for help with planning a budget.

YOUR ROOM, YOUR WAY

A detailed plan is key to the success of any room makeover. Use the following foolproof process to devise your plan.

Wish List

To ensure your room transformation plan accomplishes all your goals, start by making a simple wish list. Writing such a list can help you pinpoint how you want your room to look and function. The list can also help you decide which existing elements can stay and what needs to go.

In each episode of *Design on a Dime*, the project wish list comes from meeting with the homeowner: The owner gives a member of the team a tour of the space and explains how he or she would like to better use the room. From this meeting, the goals are defined. Chances are, you are going to tackle your room makeover yourself. If so, you can still employ the same method to help you bring focus to your mission. With paper and pencil in hand—and armed with clippings of your favorite rooms from books and magazines—take a tour of your room. What are the elements of your dream room? Even if budget or space constraints don't allow you to completely overhaul your space to match the rooms you see in print, identify the individual elements—color, types of furniture, and room layout—that speak to your functional and style needs.

For help in deciding what to put on your wish list, see Establishing Design Priorities on page 20. Once you have established what amenities you and your family require, you can move to the next phase of planning: budgeting.

Budgeting

Budgeting is easy for the *Design on a Dime* design coordinators: Each room makeover has a firm budget of $1,000. Every room featured in this book and on the show illustrates how far this amount can be stretched—often far enough to accomplish every goal outlined by the homeowner.

If you are uncertain of just how much you need to spend to create the room of your dreams, transform your wish list into a shopping

Mix form and function by displaying what you love with what you need. See pages 30–35 for more on this hardworking space.

Establishing Design Priorities

Ask yourself the following questions and you'll get a clearer picture of what you have, what you need, and what you want your room redo to accomplish. If other family members will also use the room, answer these questions together to ensure everyone's needs are met.

• How much time do you spend in this room?
• What do you do in the room? Do you eat meals or snacks, read, relax, sleep, primp, watch television, or fold laundry?
• Would it be helpful or annoying if you or other family members could access the phone or television from this space?
• Does the space function the same or differently on weekends and holidays?
• Who uses the space? You, your spouse, children, friends, extended family, colleagues, or some combination of these?
• What can be fixed or refurbished? Are there furnishings or accessories you no longer need? What needs to be replaced? What must remain in the room to meet your functional objectives?
• How does the current decor make you feel? How would you like it to make you feel?
• Is the lighting adequate during the day? At night? Does the room ever seem too dark or too bright?
• Are there specific furniture pieces that would make the room more comfortable? Can you purchase a piece of the right size from a local outlet or will you need to make it or order a custom piece?

list by replacing needs with tangible solutions. For example, change "more storage" to "four-drawer dresser," "shelving unit," or "display hutch." Then get price quotes for all the materials, furnishings, and accessories on the shopping list. The Budgeting Worksheet *opposite* provides a good starting point for this process, as well as a spot for you to add up the "hard" costs associated with your project. However, keep in mind that these numbers don't account for all costs involved in a room makeover. For instance, if you plan to hire someone to install new light fixtures, you'll need to get an estimate for the labor cost and add that amount to your bottom line.

If, after adding up all the variables, your project seems too costly, think about some possible trade-offs. Consider making changes based on a timeline (for example, you can paint the space and replace the window treatments now and update the carpeting and furnishings next year) or look for more affordable ways to get the look you want (for instance, you can slipcover the sofa instead of replacing it). One easy way to get a personalized look is to do the work yourself. In every chapter in this book, you'll learn how to maximize the impact of your decorating dollars through affordable, easy, do-it-yourself projects.

Mapping It Out

To ensure that your list of amenities will fit into the allotted space, create a scale drawing of the area. Photocopy the grid paper on page 22. Using one square to represent 1 square foot of floor space, draw the footprint, or perimeter outline, of the area you are redoing. Include details such as placement of windows, doors, stairs, pillars, the fireplace, and so on, using the architectural symbols on page 23 to indicate these features.

Measure the furnishings, cabinetry, and other elements you plan to add to the room. On another sheet of grid paper, draw these items to scale and cut out the shapes with a crafts knife or scissors. Arrange these templates on your footprint drawing to experiment with furniture arrangements and to see how well the room will function once your project is complete. (For suggested walkway clearances, advice on arranging furnishings to enhance conversation, and finding or creating a focal point for your furniture arrangement, see page 82.)

If you are revamping your kitchen on a budget, think about which elements you can add that will make the space more functional, such as a freestanding island in the kitchen *left*, and which inexpensive surface treatments—including paint and window treatments—will add a personal touch.

BUDGETING WORKSHEET

Materials to Purchase	Quantity	Cost Per Unit	Total Cost (Qty x Unit Cost)	Source/Store	Notes
Accessories					
Appliances					
Artwork					
Cabinetry					
Fixtures					
Flooring					
Furnishings					
Lamps and Light Fixtures					
Paint					
Trimwork and Moldings					
Wallpaper					
Window Treatments					

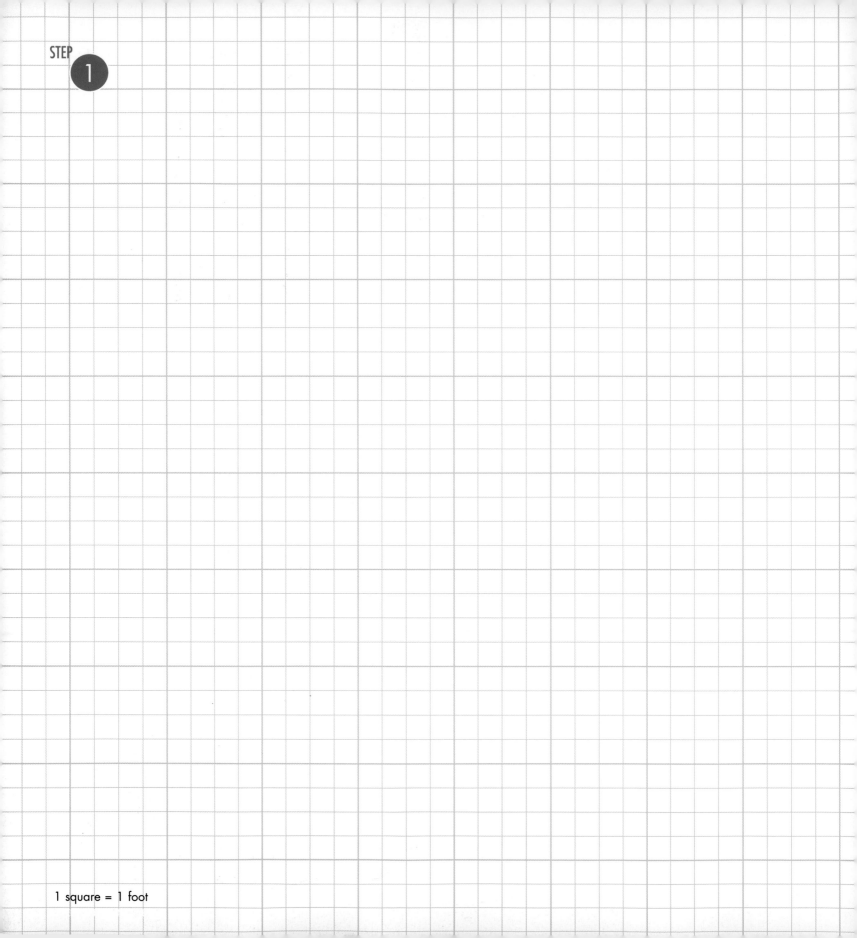

STEP
1

1 square = 1 foot

"A little money and a lot of imagination add up to a beautiful new space."
— Lee Snijders

See pages 24–29

Symbols

$ Light Switch

⊕   Light Fixture (Not Lamp)

S   Single-Pole Switch

S₃   3-Way Switch

⊤   Duplex Outlet

TV   Cable Outlet

⊤₂₀ₐ   Air-Conditioning Outlet (20 Amp)

⊙   Floor Outlet

○   Recessed Ceiling

Wall Bracket

Ceiling

Track Lighting

Telephone

Ceiling Fan

Doorbell

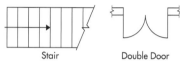
Stair   Double Door

Double-Hung Sash

Casement Sash Opening In or Out

Door Swinging In or Out

Bifold Doors

Sliding Doors – 6 or 8 Feet

Cased Opening (Passage)

Fireplace With Mantel

For more on furniture arranging, visit HGTV.com/roomplanner.

See pages 30–35.

See pages 24–29

KRISTAN

SPENCER

DAVE

Fresh terra-cotta paint warms the kitchen walls and provides eye-catching contrast with the existing white tile countertops and floors. Window coverings, custom-made by Kristan, unite wall and accessory colors.

BEFORE

KITCHEN CENTRAL

You don't have to spend a fortune to make your kitchen more functional and inviting. A few simple fixes can increase storage and work space while making the room look and feel like the heart of your home.

Design Goal

The owners of this kitchen wanted the room to feel cozy and inviting, while accommodating a multitude of activities—from daily cooking and meal service to serving as a spot for completing homework and hosting casual gatherings.

Custom Fit

As with any room where multiple activities take place, defining your requirements can help you make the room better match your needs. Ask yourself these questions: Do we need more work space? If so, where would it be most useful? Do we need more storage? (If so, for what? Dry goods, pots and pans, serving pieces, cookbooks—all of the above?) Is the storage we have as convenient and hardworking as it could be? Is the lighting adequate? What do we like about the decor? What must go? Answering these questions will help you define and prioritize your wish list.

With your needs defined, look for simple solutions. For example, a new dining hutch can store and display seldom-used dishes and free up kitchen cabinets for more frequently used items. If you don't have room for a hutch, consider installing open shelves and a plate rack near the dining table. A pot rack above a counter offers convenient storage for cookware and costs less than a new cabinet. Affordably priced ready-made appliance garages, available at home centers and kitchen supply outlets, put the backsplash to work and clear up countertop clutter.

You can also increase work space with the addition of a rolling cart or worktable. Look for ready-to-assemble kitchen carts and worktables at home centers, kitchen supply outlets, and in kitchen furnishing catalogs. For a more customized solution, consider adding a new island such as the one Dave made (see page 26).

Six Steps to Design Success

1. **Planning. The owners requested more room for dining, more convenient storage for pots and pans, more work surface, and a more inviting atmosphere.**
2. Color. Tuscan colors and distressed finishes complement the existing dark stained cabinetry and exposed beams.
3. Furniture. A new butcher-block island, bench, and bookshelves give new function to once-wasted floor and wall space.
4. Fabric. Reproduction old-world patterns reinforce a vintage European decorating scheme and soften window casings and hard furnishings.
5. Artwork and accessories. Carefully chosen pieces bring in color and texture while keeping the budget in check.
6. Lighting. Existing fixtures provide adequate ambient and task lighting. New fabric panels on the sliding glass doors pull back from the glass to prevent blocking the sunlight.

Kristan purchased this colorful serving platter for just a few dollars. The platter ties together the kitchen colors and brings a bit of artistry to the countertop.

Customize Your Kitchen

An easy-to-build center island with a butcher-block top (purchased precut from a home center) *left* puts empty floor space to work as storage and work space.

Colorful seat pads, toss pillows, and a table runner *below left, below right,* and *opposite* bring more pattern and interest to the refurnished eating area that now doubles as a homework and game center.

Because the owner is an avid collector of cookbooks, the *Design on a Dime* team filled a wall of the breakfast room with shelves. The shelving unit *below* attaches to the back of a custom bench. The hinged wooden bench seat opens to provide storage for seasonal items.

The butcher-block top was purchased precut from a home center. A wood frame (cut from Douglas fir 4×4s) and a hardwood shelf complete the project for less than $240. Hooks screwed into the underside of the butcher block hold pots and pans.

Food Service

If you need more seating around the table, consider replacing armed chairs with benches or armless versions—both take up less horizontal seating area than armed varieties. To maximize floor space, choose a table with leaves that can be folded down or removed when not in use. Shop for bargain-priced models at secondhand shops and at yard sales.

Light Source

Add more ambient lighting with a new chandelier and undercounter strip lighting. To allow in more sunlight, choose minimal window treatments such as fabric valances (see page 24). If you opt for full treatments such as shades, blinds, or fabric panels, make sure they can be pulled completely up or to the sides of the window.

Cozy Color

To make a large space feel friendly, paint the walls a warm color such as red, orange, yellow, or terra-cotta. Like the sun, these fiery hues visually heat up any space.

Soft Touch

Fabric accessories, such as chair cushions, toss pillows, table linens, and window valances, bring living room comfort to a working room. In this kitchen, padded benches combine with toss pillows and fabric-covered message boards to soften wood furnishings and fill empty walls. An area rug softens the floor.

Accessory Impact

Artwork and accessories make a kitchen feel complete. For the walls, choose items that can withstand heat and spatters, such as decorative tiles, framed prints, and colorful plates. Accent the table with a runner and a vase filled with grasses or garden flowers. For more color, layer on tablecloths or place mats and bud vases.

Project Costs

Butcher-block island, table, bench seating, chairs, and bookcase: $536

Paint and supplies: $21

Message board: $71

Fabric for pillows, cushions, and window treatments: $204

Rug: $125

Accessories (plates, table runner, wheat for pitcher): $38

Total Cost: $995

change it up

For a casual, eclectic look that appears to have evolved over time, assemble a variety of seating pieces around the breakfast or dining room table. Mix and match fabric patterns too. For more advice on pattern mixing, see page 110.

Bistro-style chairs—purchased from a thrift store—offer additional seating. The lightweight chairs can travel from place to place in the kitchen, so friends and family can always be near the cook.

MAKE A MESSAGE BOARD

Step-By-Step

1. Wrap a piece of hardboard or fiberboard with batting. Staple the edges of the batting to the back of the board.

2. Layer the desired fabric right-side up over the batting. Staple the edges of the fabric to the back of the board, stretching the fabric taut.

3. Attach the saw-tooth picture hangers to the back of the board according to the manufacturer's instructions. (Space the picture hangers to align with the wall studs.)

4. Measure and mark the wall to position nails for hanging (photo A).

5. Attach the message board to the wall with angled nails (photo B).

To make a frame for the message board, see page 47. For a more decorative look, crisscross ribbons across the front of the message board, stapling the ribbon ends to the back of the board. Secure ribbon intersections with decorative tacks; tuck drawings and photos between the ribbons.

You Will Need

Piece of hardboard or fiberboard in desired size (the one shown measures 4×5 feet)

Batting cut to the size of the fabric piece

Staple gun

Staples

Decorative fabric that is about 6 inches longer and 6 inches wider than the message board

Scissors

2 heavy-duty saw-tooth picture hangers

Hammer

2 nails

Decorative tacks

Ribbons

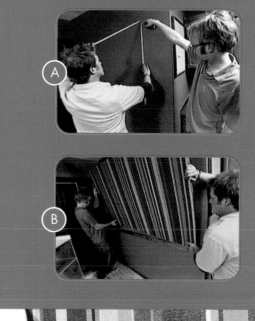

"Dress kitchen windows and furniture in colorful fabrics to add softness and create a cozier feel."
– Kristan Cunningham

KRISTAN

SPENCER

DAVE

Dual-purpose furnishings and an earthy, simple look make this small apartment function as a much larger space. Putty-color paint softens the starkness of the white walls without darkening the room.

BEFORE

STUDIO MAGIC

As this studio apartment illustrates, the right furnishings, colors, and accessories can make a small space live large.

Design Goal

The resident of this single-room home wanted a more attractive and functional layout to better accommodate everyday life, working from home, and occasional entertaining.

Planned Performance

To make the most of a multifunctional room, thoughtful planning is critical. List all the activities the space must accommodate and then choose furnishings and accessories that can serve more than one purpose. Can the sofa fold out to make a bed? Can the dining table double as a work surface? Consider tall storage units to take advantage of underutilized wall space. Keep utilitarian items behind cabinet doors and put more attractive items such as books, baskets, and vases on open shelves. For added sparkle, highlight displays with low-cost lighting strips made for shelves or with small low-voltage battery-operated spotlights. Make a side table work harder: Select one equipped with shelves or drawers. You can also skirt a table, as shown on page 35.

If you'll be working from home regularly, consider a built-in office credenza or a computer armoire. If you only need enough work space to pay bills or write letters, a simple writing desk tucked into a corner or beneath a window may be enough. A slim sofa table can also accommodate a laptop computer and a small printer.

When it comes to furniture arranging, think about traffic flow and floor space. Arrange furnishings so that they separate the room into functional areas and leave uninterrupted traffic ways between each area. Float some furnishings near the "edge" of each activity area to create more visual appeal and to take advantage of all the floor space. Angling furnishings can also make a narrow room appear wider or give a box-shape space more visual appeal.

Six Steps to Design Success

1. **Planning.** A lengthy discussion with the owner yielded a list of design priorities: Make the space look less like a bedroom and function better as a gathering and work space.

2. **Color.** Pastel walls create a more soothing ambience than the original white without closing in the space. Unifying wood tones makes the room appear more cohesive.

3. **Furnishings.** Library shelves serve as work, storage, and display space, and a new platform bed doubles as a sofa.

4. **Fabric.** A solid mattress cover and complementary toss pillows soften the look of the room without overpowering it.

5. **Artwork.** Nature photos, shot at a nearby park, connect the apartment to the neighborhood and the outdoors.

6. **Lighting.** A hanging lantern and a swing-arm lamp better illuminate the apartment when the sun isn't shining.

Originally, this vintage trestle table was pushed against the wall the long way, allowing space for only two diners. Changing the table's orientation makes it possible to seat four or five. A paper lantern hung above the table illuminates the surface for both dining and paperwork.

Details Make the Difference

Creamy white pillar candles *above* provide mood lighting at little expense. Votive candles spread across the bed shelves help unify the look of the room.

To give mismatched furnishings a more cohesive look, paint or stain each piece the same color and add matching hardware. *Above right,* bargain-priced shelves were updated with a deep walnut stain to match the stain on the owner's trestle table.

Installing a shelf between two ready-made bookshelves *right* provides a spot for the computer monitor and keyboard and makes the freestanding pieces appear built-in.

A custom headboard and footboard make the bed *opposite* look more like a sofa. Toss pillows resemble back cushions.

Valuable Assets

A standard bed, like the one shown in the Before on page 30, makes a studio space look too much like a big bedroom. A better solution is a daybed, futon, or sleeper sofa that can be pushed against the wall and double as seating. You can turn a twin or double bed into a sofa by building a platform for the mattress and adding a matching shelf-style headboard and footboard (see page 30). A plethora of pillows makes the extra depth comfortable for sitting, and the pillows can be tossed out of the way at bedtime and, if necessary, used as cushions for floor seating.

Thrift-store-purchased bookcases and a simple wooden connecting shelf combine to serve as a computer center, library, storage unit, and display spot. An existing trestle table placed opposite the bookcases functions as both a work surface and a dining table.

Shade Secrets

To keep the space from feeling too dark and cavelike, Kristan chose a light putty shade for the walls. "The color is softer than the original white, yet is still light and bright enough to make the space feel open and airy," Kristan explains. When choosing a color scheme for a small space, choose cool, pastel shades—watery blues, restful greens, and dreamy-sky violets. Unlike warmer, more vibrant hues, such as orange, yellow, and red, these low-profile colors recede into the background and make a small space seem larger. Conversely, warm tones appear to advance, making a large space feel cozier. Because this apartment is frequently flooded with bright sunshine, the soft shades also help to keep the room's visual temperature in check.

Functional accessories

Use pretty containers such as baskets and bowls to organize necessities such as pencils, stamps, stationery, CDs, and remote controls. Cover the phone book and the dictionary with a wallpaper remnant or rice paper to make them blend better with the decor.

View open wall space and empty tabletops as opportunities for personal touches. Hang framed prints, interesting pieces of architectural salvage, decorative plates, and display shelves to bring a sense of individuality to the space. Spencer shot the framed

photos *opposite top left* with a digital camera and had them enlarged. Inexpensive black plastic frames and simple white mats complete the custom artwork.

Fabric Finesse

Small print or solid color fabrics make a small space appear larger. Avoid large, busy fabric patterns as they can become unwanted focal points. For this space, Kristan chose solid fabrics adorned with simple, embroidered patterns for the toss pillows. Natural rattan shades bring a tailored look to the windows casings and connect with the outdoors.

Easy Lighting

A new paper lantern and a floor lamp provide ambient and task lighting for less than $50. Swagging a fabric-covered or chain-decorated cord enables you to create more overhead lighting without any additional wiring. Swing-arm lamps—especially halogen ones—can create ambient, task, and accent lighting for little expense. For more information on the various types of lighting, see pages 160–169.

Project Costs
Paint and supplies: $30
Couch: $206
Accents (photos): $120
Workstation: $214
Accent pillows: $141
Open shelves and accessories: $121
Rattan shades: $87
Lighting: $47
Hardware and incidentals: $31
Total Cost: $997

Make your bed look like a comfy sofa by building a platform to fit the mattress (this mattress is full-size) and adding an identical headboard and footboard that can double as display shelves. Fill the back with lots of toss pillows to add additional softness and comfort.

The wide headboard and footboard with cutout shelves function as side tables for storage and display. For special occasions, votive candles in glass holders bring festive sparkle to the room.

SKIRT A TABLE

Transform empty space into storage and give a plain table some design dash with a simple table skirt.

Step-By-Step

1. Measure the front and side edges of the table to determine the fabric width. (Because this table is pushed against a wall, the skirt only covers three sides.) Add another 4 inches for side hems.

2. Measure the length of the skirt from the top edge of the table to the floor. Add 4 inches for hems.

3. Cut the fabric to these measurements. You may need to piece fabric widths to obtain the required table skirt width.

4. To hem the top and bottom edges of the skirt, fold under 1 inch and press. Fold under 1 inch again, press, and stitch. Follow the same procedure to hem each side of the skirt.

5. Use fusible-adhesive material to adhere the ribbon to the top edge of the skirt. Apply one half of the hook-and-loop tape to the top edge of the back of the skirt.

6. Apply the remaining half of the hook-and-loop tape to the top edge of the table (photo A). Hang the skirt on the table, pressing together the two halves of the hook-and-loop tape (photo B).

> *"Multipurpose furnishings help conserve space in a small apartment."*
> – Spencer Anderson

You Will Need

Measuring tape
Fabric, matching thread
1-inch-wide ribbon
Scissors
Iron and ironing board
Fusible-adhesive material
Sewing machine
Straight pins
Adhesive-backed hook-and-loop tape

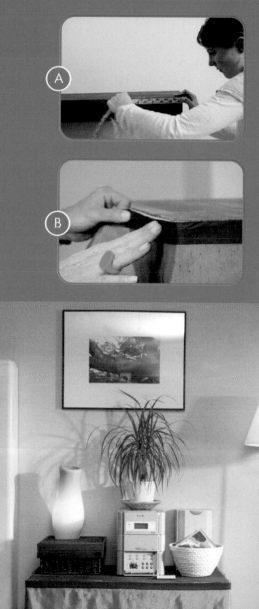

This table once served as the owner's desk. To give it new life, Kristan cut the table in half and attached it to the wall for support. A new skirt keeps videos and other media equipment under wraps.

Before the makeover, this dining room felt cold and uninviting. Furnishings and architecture were at decorative odds. Now new furnishings complement the 1930s architecture, creating a cohesive design that suits a multitude of entertaining needs.

BEFORE

DINING IN STYLE

With some creative planning, your dining space can feel as inviting for two as it does for a crowd. If square footage is limited in your home, a dining area can also be configured to accommodate a variety of activities in addition to meal service.

Design Goal

The residents of this apartment wanted their eating area to accommodate a multitude of entertaining needs, including beverage and hors d'oeuvre service. In terms of styling, the couple wanted the space, viewable from the front door, to pay homage to the 1930s era when the apartment was built.

Planned Perfection

When planning dining space, first identify how you and other family members want to use the area. Do you plan to eat dinner in the room nightly or only occasionally? How many people will be using the room on a regular basis? When you entertain, how many people will the room need to accommodate? Would the room be more valuable to you if it served additional purposes, such as a computer station, student study area, or home office?

Once you have determined how you want the room to function, identify what you need to make it function that way. For example, if you want the room to double as a study space or office, consider purchasing or building a storage armoire that can also double as a computer or writing desk. If entertaining is your primary goal, a rolling bar or buffet table could allow you to move easily from the kitchen to the dining area to the patio or the gathering room. Is your existing table the proper style and size? Would a drop-leaf table or a pair of smaller round tables better fit your needs?

As the Before photo shows, it is possible to squeeze a large table into an average-size room, but the fit looks out of balance. If you must use a large table in a smaller room, consider a glass-top one to consume less visual space. Evaluate vertical space too—because the ceilings in this room are tall, a tall hutch would also make a nice addition.

Six Steps to Design Success

1. **Planning.** Properly scaled furnishings, artful accessories, and a period light fixture complement the style and size of this dining room, while providing enough storage and service space to meet needs for entertaining.
2. **Color.** A warm 1930s palette suits the architecture of the home and provides a welcoming backdrop in this entertaining space.
3. **Furnishings.** Secondhand solid-wood furnishings look like new with reupholstered seat cushions, a fresh coat of furniture polish, and a few new decorative details.
4. **Fabric.** Silky panels and light-filtering sheers control light and soften window casings. A new area rug brings color and pattern to the floor.
5. **Artwork.** Stylized pieces are easy to make and reinforce the room's overall design theme.
6. **Lighting.** The most expensive item in the room, the period chandelier, is controlled by a dimmer switch to instantly change the mood of the room.

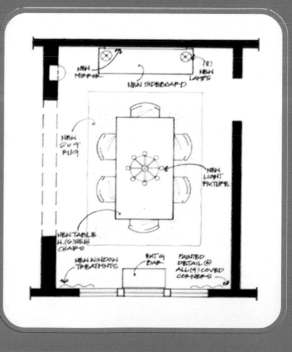

Disguise Flaws

If you find a piece of furniture that is sturdy but looking a little worn or slightly damaged, cover its flaws with decorative moldings or plinth blocks stained to match the piece. When Dave purchased this sideboard, some of the round plinths were missing. To give the piece new life, he removed all the remaining plinths (by popping them off with the flat side of a screwdriver). Next he purchased new prefabricated wooden embellishments from a home center, stained them to match the sideboard, and glued on the fresh set with wood glue. If necessary, choose embellishments that are slightly larger than the original ones to cover any dents and scratches you may make when removing the original adornments.

Match Form to Function

Original to the dining area, this simple bar cart *above* complements the new furnishings and provides additional storage for serving pieces and liqueurs. Because the piece is smaller than other furnishings in the room, Kristan balanced it between two side chairs, leaving just four chairs around the table.

The simplicity of the window treatments *above* complements the design of the newly purchased furnishings. Shirred-on-rod, honey-color crepe silk curtain panels take on a warm buttery glow when touched by sunshine. Inside-mount, ready-made sheers soften afternoon rays.

Arrange the dining table so traffic flows smoothly around it—usually near the room's center. (The exception? To turn a dining room into a multiuse space, push the table to one side to make room for a pair of overstuffed chairs or an office nook.) Plan at least 8 square feet for a table for four, plus about 36 inches so chairs can be pulled out.

Furniture Finesse

In this dining room, the original French country furnishings (see page 36 Before), on loan from generous relatives, were more ornate than the 1930s Art Deco architecture of the room dictated, and the table was too long for the room. To solve the furnishing problems, Dave went on a hunt for a secondhand table and chairs, searching local yard sales, flea markets, and antiques shops. His patience resulted in this simple 1930s-style table and six chairs, along with a generously sized matching sideboard, all purchased as a set for just $150.

Period Lighting

A contemporary track light did not complement the style of the table or the room, and the intensity of the light was too harsh. To find a fixture that was a better match, Kristan searched antiques shops and lighting outlets. Although this 1930s reproduction fixture cost more than the entire dining set, the fixture's style complements the architecture of the room and the soft, glowing light it provides is ideal for dining. Attaching the fixture to a dimmer enables the residents to instantly change the mood of the dining room to match the occasion.

Color and Fabric Highlights

In addition to identifying what your dining room needs, your plan should also include ways to spotlight amenities. For example, the charm of this room lies in its sleek 1930s styling—a classic coved ceiling, an elegant arched entrance, and stylish recessed niches—all painted white. To draw attention to these classic details, Kristan, Spencer, and Dave painted the walls with putty and nickel color paint and added a white-painted decorative molding treatment near the ceiling line. The soft colors—commonplace in the 1930s—

draw more attention to the white-painted details and bring visual warmth and charm to the room. The wood plank flooring, another charming and original feature, is accented by an intricately patterned area rug that contains all the colors used in the room's new palette. The fabric on the chair cushions complements both the rug and the wall color. For advice on reupholstering chair cushions, see page 41.

Finishing Touches

Accents and accessories make a room feel complete. Plan for them in the same way as you would all of your furnishing and lighting selections. Along one wall of this dining room, a trio of architectural photographs—shot by Spencer using a digital camera and printed out on a home computer—show off Art Deco details on downtown buildings. On the opposite wall, Kristan filled an inexpensive shadow box with antique metal backplates that once adorned the doors inside another 1930s-era home. A new mirror frame, made from low-cost medium-density fiberboard (MDF) also sports an Art Deco theme. Additional chrome and glass accessories—staples in the 1930s—decorate the tops of the sideboard and existing bar cart. A pair of pillar candles and a fresh arrangement of flowers on the dining table finish the room and give it a welcoming look.

Project Costs

Dining set: $150
Chair fabric and rug: $244
Window treatments: $48
Light fixture and supplies: $219
Paint and supplies: $42
Artwork and accessories: $248
Decorative ceiling molding: $45
Total Cost: $996

an easy match
A large tablecloth can provide just enough fabric to cover six to eight chair cushions and often costs less per yard than decorator fabrics. For more decorating finesse, purchase napkins to match your tablecloth-covered chairs.

REUPHOLSTER WOODEN CHAIR CUSHIONS

Make old wooden chairs look like new by covering the cushions with beautiful fabric. The technique is so easy you may want to consider changing the fabric each spring and fall along with other seasonal accessories.

You Will Need

Screwdrivers, flat and phillips

Fabric in desired color and motif

Optional: High-density upholstery foam and polyester batting in

desired loft, cut to fit seat; spray adhesive

Pins

Scissors

Staple gun and staples

Step-By-Step

1. Turn the chair upside down and remove the seat using the appropriate screwdriver.

2. If the original fabric and foam are in good shape, you can simply staple new fabric over the old (photo A). If the fabric and foam need to be replaced, use the flat screwdriver to remove the old staples that hold the fabric to the seat. You will use the old fabric as a pattern.

3. Lay the new fabric flat, right side down. Place the old fabric on top; pin in place and cut out.

4. To replace old foam and batting, attach new high-density foam to the wood seat with spray adhesive. Top with batting.

5. Center the foam- and batting-covered seat on the wrong side of the new fabric. Starting on one side, pull the fabric to the underside of the wood seat and staple at the center of the fabric edges. Repeat on the opposite side, then on the two remaining sides, pulling the fabric taut. Continue stapling the edges all the way around the seat (photo B.) At the corners, neatly fold and staple. After stapling is complete, trim any excess fabric (photo C).

6. Turn the chair right side up and replace the seat in the chair.

7. While holding the seat in place, turn the chair upside down and screw the cushion in place, using the appropriate screwdriver.

"Whether you choose new, vintage, or antique furnishings, look for quality construction and materials."
— Dave Sheinkopf

BEFORE

To maximize natural light without giving up privacy, Kristan covered the windows with self-adhesive translucent window film, available at most home centers. To illuminate the mirror above the sink, Spencer installed a Hollywood fixture directly above the mirror.

BATH BLUEPRINT

To make your bath as hardworking as possible, start with a comprehensive wish list, then use your imagination to transform your dreams into reality.

Design Goal

The resident of this apartment wanted a more comfortable and functional bath with a touch of Hollywood glamour and elegance.

Dream Scheme

To ensure your room makeover plan accomplishes all of your goals, you'll need to make a list of your needs and wants (see page 19 for more guidance on this step). That is especially important in the bath, the most personal—and likely the smallest—room in your home. For this space, before you think about the functional elements you require, focus on the mood you want to create. Are you looking for a place that pampers your body, soothes your spirit, or brightens your mood every time you enter it? Use your desired ambience to guide the choices you make.

Functional Form

If budget constraints prohibit you from making major structural changes (or if you are renting your home), you can easily make your bath work harder and look better with cosmetic changes. Painting the walls a dark color creates drama, while pastels reflect more light and will make your bath feel larger and look brighter. Replacing a dark vanity countertop with a white or cream color one will reflect more light up onto your face and make applying makeup and shaving easier to see. A coat of paint and new knobs can make dated cabinetry look nearly new, and adding off-the-shelf storage organizers can instantly increase cabinet storage capacity.

Freestanding Furniture

To further supplement existing storage, add freestanding furniture pieces such as a storage chest for linens (you can find them built tall and narrow or short and wide to fit most any space), a bath

---

Six Steps to Design Success

1. **Planning. The resident's desire for a glamorous Hollywood-style bath guided the design team's color, lighting, and storage choices.**
2. Color. Chocolate brown walls combine with soft blue and shiny gold accents to fill the room with color. White tile balances the dark walls and helps reflect more light.
3. Furnishings. A new padded bench creates a spot for reading and relaxing.
4. Fabric. A new sink skirt, shower curtain, and scarf valances soften the hard surfaces.
5. Artwork and accessories. A monogrammed plaque hangs on the wall above the tub and is flanked by two small shelves that hold decorative vases (see page 44). Decorative hatboxes look pretty while providing functional storage.
6. Lighting. A new chandelier and a trio of wall-mounted fixtures enhance natural light.

A wooden platform supported by pillars standing inside a porcelain bathtub covers a rust-stained basin and creates the illusion of a built-in chaise.

Movie Star Comfort

A new gathered satin sink skirt *above* softens the look of an old pedestal sink and provides undercover storage behind its gathers.

Once an eyesore, this never-used bathtub *top right* was disguised as a built-in bench. A simple wooden platform (held up by wooden pedestals inside the tub) is topped with an upholstered cushion and several toss pillows to create the look of a chaise. Five new shelves adjacent to the chaise and a new shelf above the toilet provide more storage and display space. Kristan made the decorative plaque hanging on the wall above the shelves from a round wooden disk purchased precut from a local hardware store. She primed and painted the piece, let it dry, and then used letter stencils to paint the resident's initials onto the disk.

Decorative brackets *right* give a simple shelf an elegant look.

armoire, or a freestanding towel stacker. To increase storage in this bath, Kristan, Spencer, and Dave decided to add a custom shelving unit to the open wall above the tub and stackable storage organizers to the inside of the existing cabinets.

Living Room Comfort

One of the easiest ways to soften the look of this often austere-looking space is to add upholstered furnishings that you more typically find in a bedroom or sitting area. An upholstered bench or padded chair makes putting on shoes and socks and applying makeup less of a chore. Soft, cushy rugs warm up cold and hard tile floors. The renter of this bath hated everything about the rust-stained bathtub, opting only to use the shower. To cover the eyesore tub and instill living room comfort, Dave covered the tub with a freestanding cushioned-top wooden platform that can easily be removed when the renter moves out, creating the look of a built-in chaise. To soften the appearance of the window moldings, Kristan draped a scarf valance around basic curtain rods. (One scarf was enough for both windows, so she cut it in half and hemmed the cut edge.) To bring a look of luxury to the plain pedestal sink, Kristan fashioned a skirt from washable blue satin. The skirt also increases storage, as the resident can stash plastic bins for storing a hair dryer, curling irons, and other items below the sink.

Streamline Design

Downplay utility with decoration. In this bath, pale blue decorative hatboxes adorn the new shelves and top existing built-ins, combining glamorous curves and old-fashioned appeal with clutter-busting storage. A new matching satin shower curtain keeps a plain shower under wraps, and decorative accessories, such as glass storage canisters and vintage bottles, hold necessities such as cotton balls and liquid soaps.

Project Costs
Paint and supplies: $48
Mirror makeovers and lighting: $120
Chandelier: $234
Tub bench and shelf: $194
Cabinet facelift: $41
Fabric elements: $43
Window treatments: $74
Wall shelves: $56
Storage boxes: $45
Monogram plaque: $44
Artwork and accessories: $97
Total Cost: $996

glitz and glamour

If your mirrors are framed, give them a new look with metallic gold or silver paint, available at crafts stores. Spread more glitter around the room by painting other pieces to match. The backplate of this Hollywood-style lamp fixture was originally white.

FRAME A MIRROR

Make a plain home center mirror look like a custom framed piece with decorative molding.

Step-By-Step

1. Measure the length and width of the mirror.

2. Have your local home center cut the molding to these measurements, or use a miter block and handsaw to cut the ends of the molding pieces at 45-degree angles (photo A).

3. Prime and spray-paint the molding pieces and allow them to dry thoroughly.

4. Assemble the molding pieces on a flat surface. Measure the length and width of the frame.

5. Cut the ultralight MDF to the match the outside measurements of the frame.

6. Glue the mirror to the ultra-light MDF and let the adhesive dry thoroughly (see photo B).

7. Attach the molding to the ultralight MDF using finish nails (photo C). Be sure the nails are longer than the width of the molding, but not so long that they will penetrate through the back of the MDF. Or glue the molding to the MDF.

8. Evenly space ring hangers near the top two corners on the back of the MDF and fasten them on with screws.

9. Thread picture wire through the ring hangers and twist each wire end tightly back over itself.

10. Use a stud finder to locate wall studs. Install heavy-duty picture hangers, anchoring them in the studs, and hang the mirror.

"Bring glamour to your bath with Hollywood-style lights and glimmering, gold accents." – Kristan Cunningham

You Will Need

Mirror

Tape measure

Decorative molding*

Spray primer

Spray paint

½-inch ultralight medium-density fiberboard (MDF)

Heavy-duty glue

Finish nails

Hammer or nail gun

Two ring hangers with screws**

Stud finder

Heavy-duty picture hangers

*If the molding you choose lends itself to butt joints, you can have the molding cut to fit your mirror at a home center. Basic cuts should be free of charge or done for a minimal expense. Most decorative molding, however, will require mitered joints, which you'll need to do yourself with a miter block and handsaw.

**Make sure the screws are long enough to securely penetrate the MDF and picture molding WITHOUT going through the back of the MDF.

Rich, plummy colors with gold
accents and dark wood create an
exotic look for a teen's room.

STEP

2

WORKING WITH COLOR

For a comfortable, soothing space, paint the walls deep taupe or nickel gray. To keep the mood relaxed, choose furnishings in paler shades of the same color and incorporate pillows and accessories in bolder tones for punchy accents. See pages 70–71 for more on this living room.

PERSONALIZE WITH COLOR

By understanding the principles of color, you will gain the confidence to use color like a pro.

The Color Wheel

Hold a prism to a light, and you'll cast a rainbow around the room simply by moving and rotating the prism. This mini science experiment is your first lesson in choosing color for any room of your home: When white light shines through a prism, it separates the light into a spectrum of colors, each with its own wavelength. Color occurs when light falls on an object and the item reflects the waves of a certain length, say those of blue, absorbing the rest. The color red has the longest wavelength, while violet has the shortest. The progression of color from longest to shortest wavelengths is traditionally presented as the 12 colors on a color wheel: three primary colors, three secondary colors, and six tertiary colors. Color relationships built on these color groups form the basis of color theory in design. The following is a list of commonly used terms that will come in handy as you begin exploring the amazing world of color and its uses in your home.

- **Primary colors.** Red, blue, and yellow. These colors are pure: You can't create them from other colors; all other colors are created from them.
- **Secondary colors.** Orange, green, and violet. These colors fall between the primary colors on the color wheel because they are formed when equal parts of two primary colors are combined (for instance, violet is derived from red and blue and lies between them on the color wheel).
- **Tertiary colors.** Mixing a primary color with the neighboring secondary color creates a tertiary color. With each blending—primary with primary, then primary with secondary—the resulting hues become less vivid. Red plus orange, for example, makes an orange-red color, and blue plus green yields blue-green.
- **Complementary colors.** Colors that lie opposite each other on the color wheel—red and green, violet and yellow, blue and orange—are complementary colors. For a striking scheme, combine complementary colors; this combination of a warm and cool color is energizing. These high-energy color schemes are perfect for play spaces and work areas, such as laundry rooms and craft areas.
- **Analogous colors.** If you prefer a more sophisticated scheme, choose analogous colors—those adjacent to each other on the color wheel—such as yellow and green or green and blue. These schemes work well in both gathering rooms and private areas and as transitions in connecting spaces such as hallways.
- **Monochromatic colors.** Monochromatic color schemes incorporate shades and tints of a single hue. A monochromatic blue scheme, for example, might feature navy, royal, and sky blue. Incorporating variations of a single color can be soothing and sophisticated (cool neutrals) or exciting and vivacious (variations of a hot tropical color).

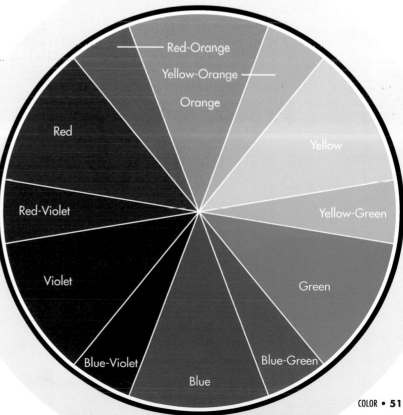

The Language of Color

- **Hue:** Hue is another word for color. It's most often used to identify a specific color, such as apple green, grass green, or pine green.
- **Shade:** A shade is a color to which black is added, taking that color from, for example, blue to navy.
- **Tint:** When white is added to a color, the resulting hue is called a tint. Add white to red, for instance, and you will shift from cherry to rose to blush pink—all tints of red.
- **Tone:** A tone or tonal value of a color refers to its intensity (or degree of lightness or darkness)—light green versus dark green, for example.
- **Chroma:** Chroma is the brightness or dullness of a color. Lemon yellow and butter yellow, for example, can have the same tone (degree of lightness or darkness), but lemon yellow would have a higher (brighter) chroma.

Combine color and texture by choosing a variety of fabric weaves and materials. For more information on fabric, see *pages 104–131.*

Warm, Cool, or Neutral?

If you've ever taken a color quiz—for selecting the makeup or clothing colors that work best for your skin and hair color—you've probably been identified as looking best in warm or cool colors. The theory behind this approach applies to home decorating too (although you don't have to paint your walls pink just because it's one of "your colors"!). Warm colors—red, orange, yellow—reside on one side of the color wheel, while cool colors—blue, green, violet—reside on the other. Blending colors can add virtual heat or chill. Green, for instance, can be warmed with the addition of some yellow—which is a good choice to take the visual chill out of a bedroom with a north-facing window. Or if you're choosing a color for a south-facing recreation room in a walkout basement, you might want to cool down your green paint with a little blue. Think of the skin of a "cool red" plum that carries violet undertones as opposed to a "warm red" you might see in a perfectly ripe tomato.

Color also has the wonderful ability to make things appear larger or smaller. Two aspects of color give it this capacity: temperature and brightness. Warm colors advance or seem closer while cool colors recede or appear farther away. Likewise, darker colors advance, and lighter colors recede. Use this to choose colors for walls, ceilings, and furnishings, and you can visually stretch or shrink elements to your liking. For example, to make a large family room seem more cozy and embracing, paint it tomato red (a warm color) or forest green (a dark color). Conversely, add some breathing room to a tiny powder room with walls and ceiling of sky blue (a cool color) or pale lavender (a light color).

The final category of colors is neutrals: black, gray, white, and brown. These versatile colors can blend into the background to let both warm and cool colors take center stage, but they can also calm dominant hues (for instance, if you paint the walls of your living room bright green, temper the color with wood tones or white-painted trim). Neutrals can be used on their own for a soothing color scheme, but to add interest, incorporate many textures—combine soft and nubby blankets with tightly woven upholstery, for example.

Black and brown calm the vibrant colors in this bedroom. See pages 62–69 for more on this space.

The yellows and oranges of a fire add visual and "touchable" heat in this predominantly neutral living room. See pages 70–73 for more on this space.

Finding Inspiration

The *Design on a Dime* design coordinators often start the color planning process with an inspirational piece in hand. It may be a favorite fabric, a hand-painted ceramic, a colorful throw rug, or a cherished piece of art displayed in the home where they are working. From this inspiration piece, the designers can determine a dominant, secondary, and accent color, and with very little effort a color palette is born. Choosing colors this way eliminates worries about whether chosen colors will match or clash. If they work together in the inspiration piece, they will work together in a room. In general, the dominant color covers 60 percent of a room (for instance the walls), the secondary color composes 30 percent of the space (such as window treatments and furnishings), and accent colors make up the remaining 10 percent (artwork, pillows, and so forth). Although you don't need to follow this formula exactly, these recommended percentages will help you determine how much of each color should be used to build a successful color scheme.

The color inspiration for a room may also come from the desire to evoke a certain ambience—lazy relaxation at the beach or the exoticism of a faraway land, for example. To find ideas, peruse books and magazines, browse at any outlet that has pieces from the place (for example, visit an import store to see the colors and textiles of India, Asia, and beyond) and, if you can't visit the locale, watch movies or TV shows to see the colors that are commonly used. To learn more about choosing great color combinations, log on to HGTV.com/color and try the Pick-a-Palette tool.

Color Insurance

Before you put a brush to a wall, purchase quarts of paint in the colors you like and apply them to primed poster boards. Place the painted boards along each wall in the room you want to paint. Review the colors throughout the day to see whether you like how the colors appear in changing light—and how they interact with your flooring, furnishings, and other existing elements. For instance, cool northern sunlight looks much different in relation to color than does strong southern light. Keep in mind that when paint covers all the walls in a room, it often appears a shade or two darker.

Correct with Color

Color can also help accentuate the architectural strengths of a room and compensate for its weaknesses. Here's how to put color to work in your home:

• **Undersize and oversize rooms.** If you want your room to feel larger or smaller, think in terms of advancing and receding colors; reds, oranges, and yellows visually advance, making walls seem closer and the room smaller. Cool colors—such as greens, blues, and violets—recede, seemingly pushing walls back and increasing the perceived size of a room.

• **Open plans.** For floor plans without obvious transitions between rooms, create planes of color to differentiate between the activities that occur in the various zones. Pick a palette of four to six similar colors, and change hues where the walls meet. The color variations create depth and contrast without jarring the senses.

• **Ceiling sensation.** Not sure what color to paint the ceiling? Consider sky blue. Nature conditions us to feel comfortable and happy when that color is above us.

"A swatch of a print fabric offers an easy way to choose a color scheme. If the colors look great together on the fabric, they will also look great together in a room." — Summer Baltzer

Shop your own home for furniture and accessories before buying new. The homeowner's sofa, love seat, and entertainment center were brought in from another room to make the family room more comfortable.

BEFORE

FAMILY COMPLEMENT

Make your family gathering spaces cheerful and inviting with complementary shades of red and green and accents of sunny yellow.

Play Favorites

One of the easiest ways to ensure you'll like your room's color scheme is to simply choose your favorite colors. The owners of this great room love deep reds and warm greens, so starting out with these complementary hues provided a simple solution to a color dilemma. Accents of yellow became another natural choice, because one of the owners collects sunny yellow firefighting memorabilia.

Opposites Attract

Hues opposite each other on the color wheel, such as red and green, violet and yellow, or blue and orange, create stimulating, high-energy spaces which provide perfect backdrops for play spaces and workout rooms. These opposite colors are riveting because, when warm and cool colors are viewed together, they seem to intensify one another, bringing out the best of both. When working with color complements, choose one shade as the "star," and let its complement work in a supporting role. This prevents the vibrant scheme from overpowering the other design elements in the room. You'll also want to bring in a neutral shade to provide some visual relief from saturated tones, as the *Design on Dime* team did here by leaving some of the walls in their original shade of medium beige. For added durability in action-packed rooms, choose a washable paint finish.

Six Steps to Design Success

1. Planning. The owners' favorite colors and firefighting-theme collectibles set the tone for a kid-friendly gathering room.
2. **Color. Complementary shades of red and green and a sunny yellow accent heat up the room.**
3. Furnishings. An existing sofa and love seat team up with new tables and an area rug to fill the sitting area with comfort and style.
4. Fabric. New curtain panels soften the look of aging vinyl blinds.
5. Artwork and accessories. Collectibles once stored in the garage fill walls and shelves with color.
6. Lighting. Lamps made from old fire extinguishers team up with existing fixtures.

Summer turned a vintage copper fire extinguisher (*above*) into a functional lamp using a lamp kit and copper plumbing pieces from a hardware store.

Personal Stamp

An antique firehouse ladder *above* hangs on the wall, along with the homeowner's collection of firefighter hats and an old soot-stained jacket, *below right*.

Vintage fire alarms and firehose nozzles serve as interesting conversation pieces when arranged in balanced groupings on tabletops *above right*.

A collection of firehouse mementos (one owner is a firefighter) adds a personal touch to this family space.

Fun and Games

Pump up the fun in your family's play space with a game table (paint a checkerboard on top of a square dining table or coffee table) and a storage spot for board games and other family favorites. Instill put-up-your-feet comfort with casual furnishings and fabrics that can withstand a shoeprint or two. In this space, the owners' air hockey table anchors one leg of the L-shape room, and a durable overstuffed leather sofa and love seat anchor the other (see page 56). Artwork and accessories should be equally as entertaining. Here bright yellow fire helmets, an old firehouse ladder, and a soot-covered firefighter's jacket increase the room's overall energy level and underscore the room's firehouse theme.

Sunny Disposition

Back up natural light with lots of overhead illumination; that way the fun will never be compromised by a lack of light. Add task lighting in areas where you'll play cards or other table games. For task lights, Summer made theme-inspired lamps out a pair of old copper fire extinguishers (see page 56–57).

Building a Display Cabinet

Charles built this display cabinet out of ¾-inch oak plywood to hold the homeowners' many firefighter-themed collectibles. Once the wood pieces are cut and assembled, everything is sanded and finished with two coats of an antique oil finish. Shelves are cut out of ¼-inch glass, and the edges are polished to make them safe to the touch. The shelves are enhanced with a spray-on decorative frosting in a simple border pattern created with self-adhesive shelf liner. The shelves are then fit into the cabinet with small brass shelf brackets.

Project Costs

Paint and supplies: $50

Furniture: $451

Lighting and accessories: $310

Brick wainscoting: $175

Total Cost: $986

make way for family

To make your family gathering spaces more kid-friendly, choose easy care surfaces, such as this ceramic tile floor, and durable upholstery fabrics that can be spot cleaned as necessary.

Pump up the fun in a family play space with a high-energy color scheme like this one. Add more durability to the walls with washable paint and wood or fiberglass wainscoting. This brick-look paneling attaches to the wall in the same fashion as standard wood wainscoting.

WARM YOUR WALLS WITH BRICK

Made from lightweight, durable fiberglass, these finished panels look more realistic than the brick paneling from days past, and they provide a great solution for covering cracked or water-stained walls.

Step-By-Step

1. Mark a level chalk line about one-third up the height of the wall(s) you plan to panel.

2. Wearing safety goggles, cut the brick fiberglass panels to height (photo A). Measure the positions of outlets on the wall; transfer those measurements to the back of each panel. Use a jigsaw to cut the holes.

3. Turn off power in the room. Unscrew and remove outlet covers.

4. Squeeze a zigzag bead of construction adhesive onto the wall side of the panel, allowing it to cure according to manufacturer's instructions.

5. Attach the panels to the wall, spacing nails along the edges of the panel as indicated by the manufacturer (photo B).

6. Use brads to nail cap molding at the top of the brick panels (photo C). If necessary in your particular installation, use a miter box and handsaw to cut the angled joints where the walls meet.

7. At each electrical box cutout, install a box extender. Replace outlet covers.

You Will Need

Measuring tape
Pencil
Level
Chalk line
Safety goggles
Faux brick fiberglass panels
Jigsaw
Screwdriver
Construction adhesive
Hammer or nail gun

Nails
Brads
Miter box
Handsaw
Finishing nails
Cap molding (enough to finish top edges of installed panels)
Electrical outlet box extenders

"Hunter green provides a cool backdrop against the warmth of the faux brick."
— Lee Snijders

Fabric panels that sweep down from the ceiling and wrap the
bedposts soften the lines of the bed and add elegance to the canopy.
A refurbished desk serves as a vanity beside the nightstand.

BEFORE

MOROCCAN DREAMS

As this teen retreat proves, you can give any room in your house a fresh new attitude by splashing color on the walls, furnishings, and accessories.

Design Goal

Originally designed for a little girl, this bedroom needs a makeover to become the hip Moroccan-style retreat its teenage occupant desires. Jewel-tone colors and intricately decorated furnishings are key to the vision.

Brush on Color

Eager to establish their own identities, teens want to give their bedrooms a personal stamp, and one of the easiest and most affordable ways to do this is with paint. If you paint the walls instead of using an expensive wallcovering, your teen can change the shade for the price of a few gallons of paint, and you won't cringe when he or she decides to tack up a poster or two. Similarly, you can update juvenile furnishings by painting drawers and adding new hardware. Make "custom" art that matches your teen's tastes by painting simple motifs onto rectangular fiberboard panels or stamping or stenciling a design directly onto the wall.

Dream Scheme

To make this once-serene girl's room feel more mature, *Design on a Dime* design coordinators Kristan, Spencer, and Dave opted to mix the existing soft blue painted walls with analogous jewel-tone furnishings and accessories. To make the scheme work, Kristan shopped for an inspiration fabric that mixed the same blue as the walls with the more vibrant tones the teen yearned for. You can gather similar inspiration for your room makeover from an upholstery fabric or window covering or from a piece of artwork or an accessory you plan to use in the space.

Six Steps to Design Success

1. Planning. Carefully chosen Moroccan-style bedding fabric bridges existing pastels with saturated jewel tones.
2. **Color. Vibrant shades create an energetic yet sophisticated ambience.**
3. Furnishings. A new vanity area provides the teen a place to apply makeup and reduces time spent in a shared bathroom.
4. Fabric. Billowing swags soften the hard lines of the vaulted room and accentuate the Moroccan theme.
5. Artwork. Painted tapestries, cutout stars, and swags of fabric fill once-empty wall space with jewel-tone color.
6. Lighting. New table lamps and a golden lantern enable the teen to match lighting to mood.

Bed pillows and toss pillows are dressed in fabrics to harmonize with the slipcover fabrics used on the sofa. Threads of blue in the bed pillow repeat the color of the walls.

Colorful Accents

Golden tassels *left,* originally designed as Christmas ornaments, dress up bedposts and visually tie the bed canopy to the other golden accessories sprinkled throughout the room.

Ribbon "hangers" *below left* give colorful painted wall panels the illusion of dimension—at first glance, guests wonder whether the tapestries are actually fabric.

This painted lampshade *below* provided inspiration for the circular stamped design on the walls *opposite.* The 12-inch sponge-painted stars *below* were cut from gypsum board, sponged with purple and gold, and hung on the wall with finishing nails. For a similar look, simply stencil a star directly onto the wall.

Textile Tenacity

The bedspread shown on page 62 provides the color combination Kristan was looking for: pastel shades of blue mixed with rich gold and deep pinks, berries, and purples. These bedding colors define the colors of the fabric swags, painted wall tapestries, and accessories used throughout the bedroom. Such saturated colors invigorate the existing pastel paint without overpowering the high-ceiling room and saved the design team hours of repainting the entire room on scaffolding.

Faux Fun

Because the walls in this room are high and virtually unadorned, the *Design on a Dime* team coordinators needed to come up with a way to give them interest without spending a fortune on new art. As a solution, each designer came up with a way to decorate the walls in true Moroccan style. For sparkle, Dave cut out eight-point stars from gypsum board and then sponged gold and berry paint onto the cutouts *opposite below right*. Nailed to the wall, the stars accentuate a freshly painted vanity.

Kristan made mock wall hangings by rolling blocks of berry paint onto several walls in the room. Stenciled and stamped designs atop the color blocks create the illusion of a fabric tapestry. A length of shimmering ribbon tacked above the painted design brings real dimension to the faux-painted wall hangings. As a final touch, Spencer hung fabric swags from plant hooks to draw the eye up to the full height of the room.

Stenciled-on stars give these built-in drawers a touch of color and style. Dave cut out the star shapes from a sheet of acetate purchased from a crafts store. New drawer pulls add more color and dimension.

Project Costs

Paint and supplies: $33
Bedding and swags: $308
Vanity seat, table, and mirror: $150
Wall stars: $60
Lamps and lanterns: $88
Knobs: $56
Loft area upholstery fabrics and furnishings: $105
Accessories: $197
Total Cost: $997

Gold-tone accessories bring grown-up glamour to the room and accentuate the Moroccan theme.

A light kit turns a candle lantern into a hanging lamp.

Mood Makers

Because the ambient lighting provided by track lights is somewhat harsh, the designers opted to create softer accent lighting. A small lantern hanging from a decorative gold chain and a pair of table lamps reinforce the exotic decorating theme. Providing accent and task lighting, the lantern and lamps create soft pockets of light throughout the day and evening.

Sari fabrics draped over a plain sofa and an unfinished table give the loft area more of a Moroccan flavor. Floor pillows provide additional seating. An old oil lamp, purchased for just $8, suggests the presence of a magical genie.

Colorful bed linens and a matching canopy make this bed look sophisticated enough for a teenager. To create a similar look in your bedroom, shop import stores and don't be afraid to mix and match linens from the children's department to achieve the color combination you are striving for.

Mounting a mirror in an import-store wooden frame with shutters creates an illusion of depth when the shutters are closed. Surrounding the piece with large cutout stars turns the vanity area into an eye-catching focal point for the room.

Two coats of oil-based paint dress a plain wooden desk in vibrant color. Gold-painted accents make the once-nondescript piece fit the room's Moroccan theme.

MAKE A FABRIC SWAG

Fabric swags bring color and softness to walls and windows and can be used to adorn headboards, accentuate artwork, disguise architectural flaws, and draw the eye to focal point areas. Here Kristan used fabric swags fashioned from $6 per yard sari fabrics (see page 121 for more information on sari fabrics) to bring more color to the walls and fill some of the room's volume.

You Will Need

36-inch or 45-inch-wide sheer fabric
Grommet kit with 1- to 2-inch diameter grommets; 6 grommets per swag
Matching thread
Scissors
Sewing machine
Pencil
Decorative plant hooks, three per swag

Step-By-Step

1. Cut fabric in lengths approximately twice the height of your wall. Note: The selvage edges can serve as the finished edges or, if you prefer, can be tucked out of sight when the swags are hung.

2. Hem the top and bottom edges of all the fabric lengths.

3. With a pencil, mark the location of the top corner grommets 2 inches in from the top corners.

4. Fold the fabric in half widthwise to find the center. Mark two points on this center line 2 inches in from the selvage edges.

5. Install two grommets at these points. These grommets will let you catch up the swag at its middle point.

6. Install a plant hook at two points at the top of the wall for the swag's starting point (photo A). Attach a third plant hook halfway down the wall where you want to catch up the swag (photo B).

7. Slip the grommets over the hooks. Shape the fabric as desired.

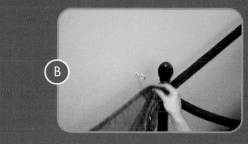

"Import stores carry products from all over the world, so they're a great place to start when you're looking for a specific ethnic theme."
— Kristan Cunningham

LEE

SUMMER

CHARLES

Custom-built display ladders flank
the fireplace and fill what was once
empty space with pattern, texture,
and dimension.

BEFORE

DESERT OASIS

To give a room that lacks personality a welcoming feel, splash earthy colors on the walls, fireplace surround, and window treatments, then toss in a few interesting accessories.

Design Goal

The owner of this living room wanted to warm this once sterile, formal space with color and life to encourage friends and family to gather in it on a daily basis.

Color Clarity

One of the easiest ways to define the color scheme for a room is to start with an inspiration piece—an object you love to look at. The color combinations found in an Asian rug, a colorful vase, or a favorite floral arrangement can point you toward harmonious color selections for the walls, upholstery, window treatments, and accessories used throughout a room or an entire home. To enliven this once-boring living area, Lee used a pair of matching botanical prints as the springboard for the room's color scheme. Paint, fabric, and accessory colors are all found in the inexpensive framed motifs. "Adding artwork or accessory items that contain all the colors in the room creates a very cohesive look," Lee explains.

Southwestern Warmth

To warm up stark white walls, Lee recommends using shades that contain red, orange, or yellow. Here clay color paint (warmed by red tones) brings a cocoonlike ambience to the living room and helps soften the intensity of sunlight that floods the room. Canyon hued toss pillows bring dollops of color to the all-white sofas; the red-orange color repeats on the window treatments, and warm putty enhances the faux-painted fireplace surround.

To accentuate a white fireplace, decorate the mantel or adorn the surround with colors that complement the walls. Here, a base coat of honey color paint was brushed over the surround's existing stucco finish and then accentuated with a ragged-on peanut butter color glaze (made from four parts clear glaze mixed with one part peanut butter color paint).

Six Steps to Design Success

1. Planning. A pair of botanical prints encompasses all the colors in the room defining the complete color scheme.
2. **Color. Canyon colors stimulate conversation and enliven the overall mood of the room.**
3. Furnishings. A new coffee table features a soothing water element topped with a bonsai cactus arrangement.
4. Fabric. Colorful curtains and a hand-painted valance soften the hard lines of the floor-to-ceiling windows and accentuate the Southwestern theme.
5. Artwork. Framed prints combine with custom-made display ladders to fill the walls with color and life.
6. Lighting. A trio of table lamps warms and brightens the space during evening hours.

Because the room is somewhat large, it felt empty even when furnished with a sofa, love seat, and club chair. Now, floor plants and accent tables fill empty corners with color and life.

Theme Scenery

Accent pieces used throughout this room help convey the owner's appreciation for primitive Southwestern design. Lee made this display piece *above* from the "scrap" landscape timber left from the ladder displays he made for the fireplace wall.

A new custom-made coffee table *above right* anchors the seating arrangement and provides a convenient spot for serving hors d'oeuvres and setting glasses. This table, made by Lee, features a flowing water element below the glass, which is an interesting conversation piece for the room.

A trio of potted plants *right* fills the display space created on these custom decorative ladders.

Living Accents

To help define your overall design scheme, choose accessories that accentuate your motif. For example, if you are creating a cottage look (as shown on pages 126–131), you'll want to choose accessories that are commonplace in these quaint, casual homes. For an Asian-inspired motif, add Oriental vases, rugs, and bamboo plants. For this space, desert succulents, cacti, and Southwestern-style pottery were chosen as the primary accessories.

Houseplants offer an easy and affordable way to bring natural color, texture, and life to any room. To stay on budget, choose small, fast-growing plants, such as a philodendron or peace plant, or theme-related plants, such as bamboo or the succulents and cacti shown *opposite top right.* For added color and design dash, paint clay pots to match your decor, or choose colorful ceramic vases to complement your scheme. In the living room *opposite bottom right,* plants in terra-cotta pots fill the ladder rungs and bring symmetry and color to the focal point fireplace.

Furniture Polish

While the white sofa, love seat, and matching chair were a part of this room prior to the makeover, they were uninspiring without a plethora of toss pillows and accent tables. To keep the budget in check, the design team purchased bargain-priced wooden accent tables and ready-made import-store toss pillows. Lee made the unusual coffee table shown on page 70 from faux-slate ceramic tiles and finish-grade plywood, and then added a flowing water element that simulates a small waterfall below the glass top.

Theme Weave

Navajo-theme stencils, which Charles made from waterproof acetate sheets, bring contrasting color to the dark rust window valances. To create a similar valance for your windows, see pages 74–75. A variety of complementary solid and Navajo-print fabrics adorn the toss pillows and bring more Southwestern flavor to the living space.

Night Light

To provide comfortable spots for reading in this enlivened living room, the design team placed traditional table lamps on each side of the sofa and adjacent to a club chair. The lamps make the room more inviting for reading and relaxing throughout the evening hours and blend with the overall design scheme.

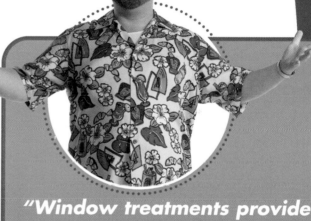

"Window treatments provide a great place to introduce color and style and help define the style of a room."
— Charles Burbridge

Project Costs
Paint and supplies: $65
Furniture: $478
Window treatments: $130
Artwork and accessories: $325
Total Cost: $998

Panels

Making curtain panels is as easy as making a valance. To combine a valance with side panels, you'll need to choose paired curtain rods designed for the arrangement. Mount the rods according the manufacturer's directions. Each panel shown is the width of the designer fabric (54 inches). The length of the finished panels is 84 inches. Adapt the length to your window, if necessary. To the finished length measurement, add ½ inch for a rolled hem and 5½ inches for the rod pocket and shirred top. For the width, measure the window width and multiply by 2; add 1 inch for the rolled side hems. Cut four fabric rectangles with these measurements to create the look shown and follow steps 3 through 5 on the opposite page for each panel. Hang the completed valance and panels on the double rods.

To warm up a large expanse of windows without blocking the light, frame the window openings with colorful panels. Here custom-made panels and a hand-painted valance combine with the existing white window sheers.

MAKE A STENCILED WINDOW VALANCE

Frame your windows in color with a custom-stenciled valance that you can make in a few hours' time. For advice on making curtain panels, see Panels opposite.

Step-By-Step

1. Mount the hanging rod according the manufacturer's directions. The length of the valance shown is 22 inches. Adjust the length to suit your window. To the finished length measurement, add ½ inch for a rolled hem and 5½ inches for the rod pocket and shirred top. For the width, measure the window width and multiply by 2; add 1 inch for the rolled side hems.

2. Cut and piece enough 28-inch-deep panels to make up the required valance width.

3. Press under double ¼-inch hems on the sides and machine-stitch in place. Repeat for the bottom hem.

4. At the top edge, press under ½ inch, then 5 inches. Machine-stitch close to the bottom fold, then stitch 2½ inches from the bottom fold to create a 2½ inch rod casing. Press the finished valance.

5. To make the stencil, adhere self-adhesive shelf laminate to a piece of poster board (photo A). The poster board provides stiffness and the laminate makes the stencil waterproof. Using a pencil and ruler, draw or trace a design onto the laminate. It should be no taller than 18 inches. Designs composed of straight lines, like the Navajo-inspired motif, will be easier to cut than curved motifs.

6. Using a crafts knife, cut out the motif (photo B).

7. Lay the finished valance on a flat, waterproof surface. Starting at one end of the valance, position the stencil, securing it with painter's tape if desired.

8. Load the sea sponge with latex paint, blotting excess paint onto a clean dry rag or paper plate. Lightly dab the paint inside the stencil cutout (photo C). Note: Charles placed a square of shelf laminate in the center of the motif as he sponged so the motif would have a red diamond-shape center (see photo D). Let the paint dry. Repeat to stencil the entire valance.

9. To set the paint, press the valance on the wrong side with a hot iron.

10. Slide the rod into the valance pocket and mount the rod.

Note: If you can't sew or don't have a sewing machine, you can use hem tape to complete this project.

You Will Need

- ½-inch diameter hanging rod with mounting hardware
- Linen or cotton fabric
- Thread to match
- Sewing machine
- Scissors
- Iron
- White self-adhesive shelf laminate
- White poster board
- Pencil
- Metal ruler
- Crafts knife
- Painter's tape
- Sea sponge
- Flat interior latex paint

Quality furnishings, such as this leather sofa and matching chairs, can last for decades. Move them from room to room as your tastes and needs evolve.

STEP

3

CHOOSING THE PERFECT FURNITURE

Purchase the best quality furnishings you can afford: Well-made, versatile furnishings are a wise design investment because they will serve you for years.

CHOOSING THE PERFECT FURNITURE

To ensure that you will be satisfied with your furniture selections for years to come, follow these simple buymanship and design strategies.

Reality Check

Before you head to the furniture store or begin perusing catalogs or Internet resources, ask yourself—and everyone in your household who will use the piece(s)—the following questions to start your search on the right foot. If you take the time to gather all this information, you'll get a clear picture of how each piece of furniture you choose needs to function. For instance, if the furnishings will be used daily—by you, kids, and pets—your furnishings will need to be sturdy, durable, and able to withstand an occasional spill. If, on the other hand, you will rarely use the furnishings and eating and drinking on them is a no-no, you'll be able to broaden your selection of furnishings to include items that are more delicate and fragile in design.

- Is your family casual or formal?
- In your household, is neatness an aspiration or an edict?
- Will you serve food or drinks in the space, or will snacks be off limits?
- Are you the rough-and-tumble type who enjoys wrestling on the sofa and jumping on a bed, or are you more careful when it comes to the care of your furnishings?
- Do you entertain a little or a lot?
- Will young children use this space frequently or hardly ever?
- Will pets be allowed in the room?

If you love a specific look, such as Asian or old-world, think back a few years. Did you love this look then? If so, you'll likely be comfortable with the look in the future. If not, limit your latest design-trend purchases to a few accessory pieces that can be replaced or updated as your tastes evolve.

The Right Fit

Just as you select clothing to fit your size, shape, and personal style, you need to do the same when choosing major furnishings. When you shop for furniture pieces, such as sofas, beds, dining tables, and armoires, take a floor plan (to make this plan, see pages 22–23), a tape measure, and fabric samples from existing pieces you plan to use in the room. Also take the wall and flooring colors. Be sure to measure openings—such as doors and hallways—leading to the room where the new piece will reside to ensure you won't have difficulties moving the furniture into the room.

Traditional pieces, such as wicker chairs and love seats, never go out of style. See page 96–103 for more on this sunroom.

Building Blocks

When buying furniture, keep longevity and flexibility in mind: You are more likely to keep furnishings that will suit more than one decorating style and can be arranged in more than one way. For example, the armoire you buy for china storage in the dining room today can be used for clothing storage in a baby's room down the road. Similarly, upholstered pieces that feature classic lines and neutral fabric can be used in different rooms to meet changing needs and tastes simply by adding colorful throw pillows, decorative throws, and even a slipcover.

Take a Test Drive

If you're shopping for an upholstered piece, sit on it and lean on it to test for comfort. If possible, turn it over to check construction (some furniture stores may have a cutaway model of the frame and cushions available for you to examine). Frames should be kiln-dried, seasoned hardwood joined by dowels or interlocking pieces, not butted together and stapled or glued. High-quality upholstery cushions have steel inner springs similar to a mattress. These springs are generally covered with a plain fabric then wrapped with polyester or down batting, a layer of polyurethane foam, and a muslin cover. A decorative upholstery cover zips over all of this. Medium-quality cushions are made from a solid piece of polyurethane foam covered in polyester batting. A muslin cover is sewn over the cushion, then the decorative upholstery cover is zipped in place. When made from high-quality foam, cushions can last for years. Lower on the quality scale are cushions made from a single piece of polyurethane foam with a decorative cover sewn permanently in place.

If you can't see the construction of a piece, avoid furniture that shows buckling between parts—cushions and frame, fitted pillow and arm, or wooden and upholstered parts. Squeeze the padded areas; you shouldn't be able to feel the frame. A sofa should never sag in the middle (indicating a lack of springs or proper bracing). (For information on upholstery fabrics, see *pages 108* and *111*.) Buy the best you can afford: These purchases will be the building blocks around which your room design evolves. Side tables, storage pieces, and accessories can be added over time.

SHOP SMART WORKSHEET *Function and Comfort Pieces*

Materials to Purchase	Quantity	Cost Per Unit	Total Cost (Qty x Unit Cost)	Source/Store	Notes
Armoire					
Bed					
Chaise					
Chest of Drawers					
Desk					
Dining Chairs					
Dining Table					
Dresser					
Entertainment Center					
Hutch					
Love seat					
Ottoman					
Settee					
Shelving Units					
Side Chair					
Sofa					
Other					

Mix and Match Prices

A high price doesn't necessarily mean high quality. Refurbished secondhand finds and unfinished pieces may be of equal or higher quality than some new furnishings. By mixing a few finely crafted new pieces with a variety of bargain buys, you'll create an interesting and individual look that seems to have come together over time rather than being purchased all at once from one source.

Look for ever-stylish pieces, such as this wicker furniture set, at secondhand shops, tag sales, and estate sales.

Comfortable Arrangements

Once you have purchased the basic furnishings for your room makeover, you'll need to focus on their placement. How you arrange the furnishings influences both the comfort level and appearance of each room in your home. Follow these guidelines for creating a smart arrangement:

• Find the focal point. A furniture grouping should be anchored by some dominant element in the room. An architectural feature, such as a fireplace, a built-in, or a window, is a natural focal point; in rooms without a dominant structural feature, create a center of interest with a large armoire, hutch, art arrangement, or bookcase (see page 76).

• Avoid lining up furniture along the walls. Even in a small space, pulling the furniture away from the walls and grouping seating pieces around a center table promotes a more comfortable conversation area. Position chairs and sofa no more than 8 feet apart to allow for easy, intimate conversation.

• Form a natural path. When placing furniture, think about how traffic will flow into and around the conversation area. Avoid cutting a path through a conversation area; instead look for ways to direct traffic along the outside of the grouping.

• Add tables and lamps. Once you have the major furniture pieces positioned, turn your attention to the pieces that will fill in your furniture layout. If possible, position a table within arm's reach of each seating piece. Choose side tables that are about as tall as the arm of the chair or sofa. Allow enough space for movement between a central coffee table and adjacent seating by placing the table 14 to 18 inches away from the surrounding sofas and chairs. For reading comfort, place a lamp near each seating area. If you have two lamps, place them diagonally across the room. If you have three lamps, create a triangle to ensure aesthetic balance and an evenly lit space. (For more information on lighting a room, see pages 160–181.)

SHOP SMART WORKSHEET *Accent Pieces*

Materials to Purchase	Quantity	Cost Per Unit	Total Cost (Qty x Unit Cost)	Source/Store	Notes
Accent Table					
Art Stand					
Baker's Rack					
Bedside Table					
Buffet Table					
Coffee Table					
Floor Lamps					
Plant Stand					
Table Lamps					
Other					

"Choose your furnishings based on the size of your family, your lifestyle, and your decorating tastes. For multipurpose spaces, use double-duty pieces—sofa beds, coffee tables with storage drawers, and generous-size tables for dining and deskwork—to boost the function." – Charles Burbridge

Before the makeover, this room was filled with mismatched furnishings in a smattering of styles. Now a cohesive old-world theme ties all the individual elements together.

BEFORE

INTERNATIONAL SUITE

Furnish your bedroom with pieces you love and create a vacation paradise at home.

Design Goal

The owners of this bedroom wanted a cozy seating area, a luxurious focal point bed, and a place to display their favorite travel memorabilia.

Vintage Finds

You can furnish your bedroom in style without breaking your budget by shopping at secondhand shops and home centers. (Then use your savings to travel as the owners of this location do!) For this suite, Charles was able to purchase two vintage leather chairs for less than $40 each by bargaining with the owner of a vintage furnishings store. A trio of tables—one for each side of the bed and one between the two chairs—was purchased new for a total of $200.

This for That

When shopping for new pieces, check home centers and discount department stores first. As you walk down the store aisles, look at items for what they could be, not for what they are. In this bedroom, Lee used a decorative folding screen purchased from a local import store as a headboard for the bed. The screen complements the style of the couple's collectibles and helps instill a cohesive feel. For advice on making a headboard from a decorative screen, see page 89. A pair of jar candles attached to this custom headboard serve as mood enhancing wall sconces.

If you prefer a softer look for the bed, think about using a cushy comforter as a covering for a padded headboard. For shelving, consider using a flat panel cabinet door as an individual shelf; because these doors are made in a variety of sizes, you may be able to find just the size you need. Embroidered towels look great when used as upholstery fabric for a bathroom cornice.

Six Steps to Design Success

1. Planning. Mixing and matching existing pieces with vintage bargains and new items fills the suite with comfort and style.
2. Color. Warm, golden tones complement the owner's color choices in surrounding rooms and gives the suite an intimate feel.
3. **Furnishings. An elaborate headboard makes the bed a focal point.**
4. Fabric. Tactile bedding and a faux-fur throw create richness and warmth, and pattern choices carry out the old-world theme.
5. Artwork. Framing an old map the owners picked up on a recent trip fills one wall with color and showcases a favorite find.
6. Lighting. Secondhand lamps team with the existing overhead fixture to fill the room with the appropriate amount of light.

Chocolate brown curtains were a given for the room. To tone down the contrast with the white cornice board, Summer painted the cornice brown and added a fabric insert made from the same pattern as some of the bedding.

Personal Showcase

A niche above the entrance to the master bath *left* provides a spot for the homeowners' travel collection. When filling a ceiling niche like this in your home, choose large displays pieces that can be easily seen from floor level and group items in separate arrangements to create visual balance as shown. For more information on displaying artwork and accessories, see pages 141–159.

Secondhand leather chairs combine with the owner's vintage Mongolian folding door *opposite* to bring a cozy look to this corner of the room. The doors were a prized possession of the owners, but they had no real purpose in the room's original design scheme. Lee used the doors as the decorating inspiration for the room, evolving all the new elements around the style of the doors.

Custom Topper

Customize a wooden valance with a fabric-wrapped foam-core board. Cut foam-core board to fit between the decorative moldings *right*, cutting separate pieces for the front and sides of the cornice box. Wrap fabric around each piece and secure it on the back with duct tape (photo A). Use adhesive-backed hook-and-loop fastening tape to attach the upholstered foam-core boards to the valance (photo B). That way you can change the covering seasonally.

Sitting Pretty

If you've always wanted a sitting area in your bedroom but are not sure you have the space, measure the dimensions of a furniture piece (or pieces) that will fit in your spot and mark the area on the floor using low-tack painter's tape. Do you like the fit? If so, shop for pieces no larger than your tape outline. If the taped area is too small for a chaise or a chair or two, think about how you could arrange the room to create more space. Could a dresser be moved into a closet or hallway? Could the bed be angled in a corner to allow for a corner seating area opposite it? Would a narrow bench fit against the foot of the bed?

An empty corner near the entrance to the bath provides the perfect spot for a sitting area in this suite. The "screen" behind the chairs is actually a vintage Mongolian folding door the owners found at an antiques shop.

Color Connection

If you've amassed a collection of furnishings that don't seem to match, unify them with color and fabric. Here wall color, bedding, sconces, and the chairs' toss pillows are all covered in warm golden tones. To make the white lamp shades a better fit, Summer coated them with an Earl Grey tea stain.

Personal Treasures

Use artwork and accessories and more fabric to transform the space into your personal paradise. If you love wildlife, for example, frame and hang your favorite watercolor renditions and then toss a few zebra pillows on the bed. If you're an amateur photographer, fill the walls with your favorite shots. As shown *opposite top left,* a once empty niche near the ceiling line now serves as showcase for the owner's collection of vases, statuary, and leather goods. For advice on lighting a bedroom, see *pages 176–179.*

Project Costs
Paint and supplies: $79
Headboard: $170
Side tables: $200
Lamps: $50
Vintage leather chairs: $80
Bedding and cornice update: $224
Artwork and Accessories: $99
Beaded valance: $96
Total Cost: $998

MAKE A FOLDING SCREEN HEADBOARD

Give your bed a bold new look with a headboard made from a decorative folding screen. For dozens of other custom headboard ideas, visit HGTV.com/headboards.

Step-By-Step

1. Remove the hinges from the decorative screen and lay the panels facedown on a flat surface with the edges butted together.

2. Measure the height of one panel along the edge. Cut four 1×4s to this length.

3. Stain the 1×4s to match the screen (this will disguise the screen's seams). Attach two of the boards to the back of the screen panels over the butted edges, using flathead screws (photo A).

4. Attach the two remaining 1×4s to wall studs, using L brackets. Stain the inside edges if not already stained (photo B).

5. From the 2×6, cut two 3-inch-long pieces. Position the pieces on the center panel about 12 inches above the floor (or at a height appropriate for your bed frame). You'll secure the bed frame to these pieces.

6. Lift the screen into position, aligning the sides of the screen with the side supports on the wall (photo C). Drilling from the outside edge of the supports, secure the screen to the supports with flathead screws (see photo D).

> **"Transform a king-size bed into a decorative focal point by adding a large, ornate headboard."**
> — Lee Snijders

A

B

C

D

Before the makeover, this space *right* lacked personality and was used more as a storage place for books than as a spot to enjoy reading them. Now the room serves as a cozy den that encourages lounging and relaxation. The furnishings are positioned to create an inviting conversation area.

BEFORE

FURNISHING FOR FUNCTION

Do you have a room in your home that could be put to better use, such as a dining area that has never hosted a meal but could be the perfect spot for a sitting room? Read on to find out how the Design on a Dime team turned a seldom-used living room into a cozy library. Furniture plays a starring role in this newly designed space.

Design Goal

Although labeled as a formal living room on the original home plan, this small room needed to serve as a cozy gathering space where the owners could enjoy a favorite pastime—reading—and conversation.

Dollars and Sense

Ask any *Design on a Dime* design coordinator how to maximize a decorating budget, and he or she will tell you to use as many existing elements as you can in your new design. When Lee, Charles, and Summer evaluated how they could transform this living space into a cozy den, they saw that the room already had a lot going for it: fine leather upholstered pieces, two light-catching windows adorned with quality plantation shutters, and plenty of lamps, artwork, and accessories.

It makes sense to work these existing functional elements into a new design so that the majority of the design budget can be spent on what the room really needs; in this case, a desk and library-style shelving. Because custom shelving units would not fit into the team's $1,000 budget, Lee purchased inexpensive ready-made shelving units and a hutch-top desk; he gave each piece a custom look by adding crown molding purchased from a home center. (For easy-to-follow instructions, see page 95.)

Making Arrangements

To maximize book storage, bookshelves line the longest uninterrupted wall and flank one of the two windows. A desk snuggles between the shelves *right*, providing a comfortable spot for paying bills. The owners' existing upholstered furnishings are

Six Steps to Design Success

1. Planning. Lee, Charles, and Summer transformed a rarely used living room into a reading den and home office by introducing better organization with a more functional layout, and by creating an old-English ambience.
2. Color. A warm, rustic color scheme and a glazed wall finish instantly add warmth to the room.
3. **Furniture. Bookcases and a hutch-top desk organize a collection of books and accessories. Moldings from a home center give inexpensive poplar wood shelving units the look of fine furniture. Put-up-your-feet furnishings encourage relaxation. A smart furniture arrangement maximizes floor space.**
4. Fabric. Durable, overstuffed leather furnishings—already a part of the furniture repertoire—ensure comfort and durability. Fringed floral-print throw pillows soften the look of the leather and wood and create a visual tie between the wall finish and furnishings.
5. Accessories. Open shelves provide space for coordinated displays of artwork and accessories.
6. Lighting. Existing reading lamps and hanging light fixtures combine with a new desk lamp and lighted art displays to make reading and desk work as comfortable as possible.

Turn ordinary bookshelves into extraordinary display cases with inexpensive molding *above*. The dressed-up shelving units display books and mementos in style.

Individual Style

You can soften masculine furnishings—such as this dark leather piece *left*—by tossing on a floral-print pillow adorned with colorful fringe. Choose fabrics with prints that tie together all the colors in the room.

The most interesting rooms are those that have a personal stamp. Lamps can offer a unique way to display your tastes and interests. This carved walnut lamp *below* and *opposite* is the perfect complement to the old-English decorating scheme in this living-room-turned-office.

The stained-glass piece *left* is a rendition of the "Jack" playing card (Jack is the first name of one of the homeowners).

Lighting Stained Glass

To give stained-glass artwork more prominence, illuminate it using Summer's foolproof method. Purchase rope lighting from a home center the same length as the perimeter of the art piece. To diffuse the light, wrap the rope lighting in photographer's diffusion film, available at a photo supply store. Attach the diffusion film to the frame using a staple gun (photo A). Fold over the excess diffusion film to hide the rope lighting (photo B) and staple it to the frame, taking care not to staple through the rope lighting. Paint the electrical cord to match the wall.

arranged in a U-shape to create a comfortable seating arrangement. A glass-top rectangular coffee table centered between the leather pieces anchors the conversation grouping.

Color Connections

To warm up stark-white walls, Charles rolled on a base coat of caramel color paint mixed in a 1:1 ratio with clear glaze. Once it was dry, he brushed on a coat of amber color glaze and then rubbed some of the topcoat off with lint-free rags. This creates a translucent finish that gives the walls a look of depth and age. The golden wall color complements the mellow tones of the bronze leather upholstery, the tobacco color shelves, and the hunter green shade of the existing carpeting.

All three colors are found in the fabric used on the throw pillows, which Summer created from an expensive vintage-look fabric. Pillows are an affordable way to use pricey fabric.

Accessory Shuffle

A mix of new and existing accessories combine with the owners' prized collection of books to fill the shelves in classic style. Heavy, curvaceous accessories are mixed between the rectilinear rows of books for variety and interest. Open areas on several shelves provide spots for the eye to rest. (For more information on arranging accessories and creating visual balance, see pages 132–139.)

Illuminating Idea

Table lamps, an old-fashioned hanging light fixture, and a desk lamp maximize reading comfort and reduce eyestrain. The lamps are placed in a triangle shape to more evenly illuminate the space. (For more information on choosing light fixtures, see pages 162–171.)

Project Costs
New furniture: $704
Accessories and lighting: $207
Paint and supplies: $83
Total Cost: $994

CUSTOMIZE A BOOKSHELF

Take a basic bookshelf from boring to beautiful with molding that is readily available at home centers. Molding—which you can easily paint or stain—comes in various widths and an astonishing range of styles, so you are sure to find one to complement the style of your furnishings. Lee purchased poplar crown molding with a reeded profile for this example.

Step-By-Step

1. Determine where to attach molding to your bookshelf (for instance, along the top edge or down the sides). Measure the areas and record the measurements.

2. Use a table saw to cut the molding to the measurements recorded in Step 1.

3. If the bookshelf is already finished, stain the molding to match the bookshelf, using as many coats as needed to obtain the right color. If you have an unfinished bookshelf, stain the bookshelf and the molding to match. When staining, wear rubber gloves and follow the manufacturer's directions.

4. Using wood glue, adhere the molding to the bookshelf (see photo A); let dry. Use a rubber mallet and finishing nails to reinforce the glue (see photo B). Don't use a hammer to set the finishing nails because a hammer may dent the molding surface.

"Adding decorative molding to plain, inexpensive bookcases creates a fine furniture look for a very affordable cost."
— Lee Snijders

You Will Need

Tape measure
Pencil and paper
Bookshelf
Molding
Table saw*
Stain
Clean lint-free rags
Rubber gloves
Wood glue

Rubber mallet
Finishing nails

*If you don't own a table saw, have your molding cut at the home center. Basic cuts should be free or done for a minimal charge.

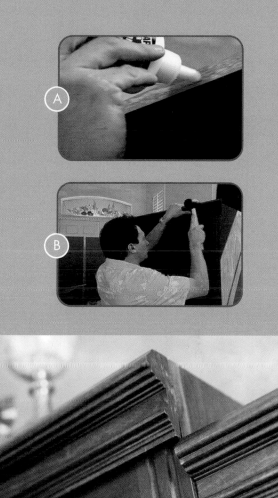

When furnishing your room on a budget, use your imagination. Here bed sheets now serve as window treatments, and wicker baskets double as chandeliers.

BEFORE

SUNNY OUTLOOK

Furnish your sunroom and other gathering areas with accommodating and stylish furnishings.

Design Goal

The owners of this sunroom wanted the underutilized space to serve two primary purposes: as a place to gather with friends after dinner and as a tranquil retreat for enjoying the sunshine and views.

Appropriate Attire

When choosing furniture for your home's gathering areas, such as living rooms, family rooms, or sunrooms like this one, think about how often the room(s) will be used and for what purpose. If you use the space for entertaining, you'll want to have enough seats for everyone. If your family gathers in the space to watch videos or TV, choose furnishings geared toward comfort, such as long sofas where you can sprawl out together or a cushy easy chair and ottoman for each family member. If you want to use the space for reading and enjoying the view, choose a cozy chair to place near a window and floor lamp.

Traditional Twist

Located just outside the bedroom door, this empty sunroom needed to be cozy enough for a couple and accommodating enough for several guests. To achieve those goals, Lee, Charles, and Summer decided to purchase a set of classic wicker furniture to fill the space. Instead of spending the majority of the $1,000 budget on the wicker pieces, Charles found a pair of secondhand chairs and a matching wicker sofa and coffee table for just $175. Then they spent a few hours repairing missing cane (see Cane Repair on page 101) and spray-painting the pieces black.

Total Contrast

To maximize light reflection in the window-clad space, the design team opted to keep the walls their original white. The secret to making a white-walled room cozy and inviting, Summer says, is to

Six Steps to Design Success

1. Planning. Because there was nothing in this sunporch the owners wanted to keep, budget conscious buying was top priority.
2. Color. White walls remained unchanged to maximize sunlight reflection. Wicker furniture was painted black to create a classic black and white color scheme.
3. **Furnishings. To maximize the design budget, the team decided to furnish the room with secondhand wicker furniture.**
4. Fabric. A set of sheets, purchased on sale, provided enough fabric for window coverings, toss pillows, and upholstered wall panels.
5. Artwork and accessories. Framed floral prints were purchased from a discount store and highlighted with fabric-covered panels. Baskets, candlesticks, console tables, and imported vases fill the room with additional texture and color.
6. Lighting. A pair of affordably priced table lamps, chandeliers made from bargain-price baskets, and picture lights supplement sunlight.

To warm up the mostly black and white design scheme, Summer chose red and green accent fabrics. She made these pillows and art accents and the Roman shades *opposite* from a set of matching sheets.

More from Less

Inexpensive baskets provide attractive storage. This basket *left* holds enough firewood for a three-hour fire.

A white mirror and candlesticks create a traditional, symmetrically balanced mantel display *below left*.

Located on a console table near the fireplace, this decorative box *below* provides storage for matches and other fireplace necessities. Additional boxes and baskets around the room keep clutter under wraps.

When furnishing your room on a budget, use your imagination. Here nested wicker baskets double as chandeliers *opposite*.

fill the walls with artwork. For this space, she chose classic black and white floral prints to play up the black of the wicker and the white of the walls. To heat up this cool look, Lee chose a rustic red and green stripe fabric (originally part of a bedsheet set) for the window treatments. The green stripe in the fabric supplies the color for the wall panels, upholstered rectangles that hang behind each black and white print to give each photo more prominence. The same stripe and solid-color fabrics were used for accent pillows on the sofa and chairs.

Light Show

To light the room during the evening, the design team purchased a pair of lamps with wicker lampshades. To create overhead lighting, Lee made "basket chandeliers" by installing light kits inside pairs of concentric baskets. Picture lights attached to each piece of art provide accent and mood lighting.

Textural Variation

An array of accessories heightens textural contrast and makes the room feel inviting to the touch, as well as to the eye. A sculptured area rug contrasts with the smoothness of the floor tile, while leather storage boxes and woven rattan baskets offer tactile contrast to the smooth ceramic vases and glass candleholders and mirrors. To complete the accessorizing, potted plants provide a natural connection to the outdoors.

Project Costs
Wicker furniture: $175
Console tables: $66
Mantel makeover: $200
Fabric (bedsheets): $60
Accessories: $220
Wall art: $125
Lighting: $150
Total cost: $996

While the budgeting mantra for an affordable room makeover is to use what you have in more interesting ways, this room had no furnishings to start with. To make the $1,000 budget stretch enough to furnish the entire room, Charles hunted down a secondhand wicker set and then repaired and painted it to make it look like new.

Cane Repair

As rattan or wicker furniture ages, the cane wrapping becomes brittle and eventually breaks. To repair missing cane, purchase caning from a wicker supply store. Soak the caning for at least 15 minutes in a bowl of warm water until it's soft and pliable like rope. Cut a longer piece than you think you'll need. Tuck the wet cane into the area vertically (photo A), then wrap the cane around the exposed area, working from bottom to top (photo B). Cut the cane and tuck the excess behind the newly wrapped area (photo C). Clamp the tucked portion (photo D) and let dry.

Picture lights accentuate the wall art displays. To avoid cords, choose battery-operated models.

MAKE AN UPHOLSTERED WALL PANEL

Solid-color fabric-covered panels accentuate framed art in this cheerful sunroom. The panels could also serve as stand-alone art if covered with a geometric print, a traditional toile, or a sunny floral pattern.

Step-By-Step

1. On the back of the plywood, align the 1-inch edge of the 1×2s with the edges of the plywood (see photo A). Screw in place to make a frame.

2. Spread the batting on a flat surface. Lay the plywood on the batting, frame side up. Pull the batting to the back of the plywood rectangle and staple it to the frame.

3. Spread the fabric on a flat surface, right side down. Center the batting-covered frame on the fabric. Pulling the fabric tightly to the back of the plywood rectangle, staple the edges to the frame (see photos B and C). Trim excess fabric.

4. Attach saw-toothed picture hangers to the frame, spacing them to align with wall studs.

5. Turn the board faceup and center the artwork on it. Mark the position for the nails, then hammer two nails into the front of the board, angling them slightly upward.

6. Hang the board on the wall.

7. Hang the framed art on the nails in the front of the board.

"Brighten a sunroom with creamy white walls and add color with furniture and accessories."
— Lee Snijders

You Will Need

¼-inch plywood rectangle cut 10 to 12 inches larger than the framed art you want to highlight

1×2s cut to fit the length and width of the plywood rectangle

Screws and screwdriver

Batting

Decorative fabric that is approximately 6 inches larger all around than the plywood rectangle

Staple gun and staples

Scissors

2 heavy-duty saw-toothed picture hangers

Hammer

Nails

A

B

C

Running the designer fabric down the center of the bedspread and canopy allows a relatively small amount of fabric to have maximum impact.

STEP

4

DECORATING
WITH
FABRIC

FOOLPROOF FABRIC STRATEGIES

The right combination of patterns, textures, and colors of textiles ensures a stylish look in any room.

Personality Match

Like people, different types of fabrics display different personalities; some are more formal, some are more casual, and some look at home wherever they go. For a listing of the most popular fabric types and their decorating attitude—as well as the types of fibers that compose these fabrics—see the chart on page 111. Use this information when shopping for upholstered furnishings or fabric accessories to freshen your home.

Material Matters

The fabric you choose for your window dressings and upholstered furnishings affects the overall appearance of your room as much as any other design component. If you love an expensive designer fabric, make the most of it by reserving it for accents, such as throw pillows, table runners, and valances. Then choose less costly decorator fabrics for sofas and drapery panels.

Although more expensive than garment fabrics, decorator fabrics have higher thread counts, tighter weaves, and more weight for longer wear, which makes them a smart buy for items that will be used frequently. If you are planning to make some of the fabric elements in your room yourself, choose decorator fabrics. Because decorator fabrics are sold in 54-inch widths, you also need less yardage than with standard 45-inch-wide garment fabrics. Note that the type of fiber and the weave you select also affect how your furnishings and window treatments wear.

Adding fabric to outdoor gathering spaces instantly increases comfort. The patterned fabrics used for these furnishings *right* and *opposite* define the color scheme for the outdoor space.

The incised wood details on this chair frame are intricate; the solid-color cushion fabric doesn't compete with the pretty carving.

> "Give a room a seasonal update with simple slipcovers and an art or accessory update."
> — Dave Sheinkopf

Upholstery Selections

The fabric of an upholstered piece is the most visible sign of quality and also the part most likely to show wear or age. Fabric cost and grade do not necessarily reflect quality. For instance, a lower-cost and lower-grade canvas is likely to be more durable than a more expensive but lighter-weight damask. Heavy fabrics, such as canvas, tapestry, woven wool, natural and faux suede, and leather, are generally more durable than lightweight fabrics, such as satin, taffeta, chintz, and linen. Plush and napped fabrics may crush with wear. Textured weaves and subtle patterns help hide dirt and soil. Keep all these guidelines in mind when choosing furnishings that best suit your needs and lifestyle.

For a fail-safe decorating plan, choose a durable neutral-color upholstery fabric that features a subtle pattern or texture. You can then "pop" the color palette by painting the walls and adding an array of throw pillows and other colorful decorating accents.

Pillow Toss

Add color and texture to your decor with a stack of throw pillows. Toss a matching pair on a sofa or love seat; for more color, step up to three or even five pillows. Mix and match florals, plaids, checks, and solids. To ensure fabrics complement one another, choose patterns of different sizes and use color as a unifying factor. You can give purchased pillows a personalized look with buttons, bows, ribbons, or fringe—and you can make old pillows look like new by slipping them into tailored button-down shams, which are available at discount stores.

A mix of solid-color and patterned fabrics— including plaids, stripes, and florals—enhance the cottage look of this living room.

You can mix patterned fabrics in a room as long as they share a common color, like the dotted bedding and striped pillow fabrics here.

Pattern Harmony

If you are having difficulty choosing a color scheme for your room, first find a fabric you love. Choose one fabric pattern that's strong enough in color or large enough in scale to carry the room. Paint the walls in a dominant or secondary hue picked from the fabric palette. Once you've chosen the wall color, go back to the fabric and find a second color to use on large upholstered pieces. Finally look for the strongest hue in the fabric pattern and use it for a few accent pillows and accessories.

For a more dynamic fabric selection, mix three patterns of varying scales. Start with a favorite print, and then work in color-related fabrics in two other scales. Love a narrow stripe? Mix it with a large-scale floral and a midsize stripe, for example. A small check also works well with a large stripe and a midsize floral.

Not sure of your pattern selections? Head to a wallpaper retailer and flip through the sample books. Wallcovering manufacturers often pair three patterns of varying sizes together; these trios typically include both wallcoverings and fabrics. Choose one of these preselected trios or simply use the samples as inspiration for your own personal look.

"Fabrics not only introduce comfort; they also add a soft touch to hard-line architecture, such as window and door frames."
– Charles Burbridge

POPULAR FABRIC WEAVES

Weaves	Description	Sample	Weaves	Description	Sample
Canvas or sailcloth	These heavy cotton fabrics are especially durable and affordably priced, but the matte surface tends to show grime; the heavy weave may hold dirt particles.		**Muslin**	Also known as voile, classic and casual muslin is woven from cotton with a texture that ranges from coarse to fine. This fabric is affordably priced.	
Chintz	The tight weave of this lighter-weight cotton helps resist soiling; spills bead up so they don't soak into the fabric. Generally, chintz is patterned, hiding small stains or dust.		**Satin**	Made from silk, linen, or a cotton weave, satin features a glossy finish on the right side and a dull finish on the back. Satin looks great in formal spaces.	
Corduroy	This casual, medium- to heavyweight brushed cotton fabric features a ribbed design and is most often used for bedding, window treatments, and upholstery.		**Sheers**	Sheers are any soft, translucent fabric that vary in opacity and gently diffuse light. They are a popular choice for under-curtains in rooms of any style.	
Damask	Made from a weave of cotton, silk, or wool, damask is known for its textural contrast between a matte finish and a satin-raised design. Damask looks best in formal settings.		**Tapestry**	This heavy woven cloth works well in both casual and classic settings as window treatments or upholstery. Tapestry features a pictorial design that disguises stains and dirt.	
Lace	Made from cotton or a cotton-polyester blend, lace features a crochetlike or eyelet design and is a popular choice for window treatments and tablecloths.		**Toile**	A tightly woven cotton with a pastoral scene, toile is a favorite in French country design. This fabric can be used for everything from upholstery to wallcoverings.	
Moiré	Made from silk or a synthetic, moiré has a finish that resembles watermarking. It is typically used for fancy window dressings, bedding, and decorative accessories.		**Velvet**	Woven of silk, cotton, linen, rayon, wool, or blends, velvet has a furlike feel. This heavy fabric blocks both drafts and light and is an ideal window covering	

Fiber Types

Synthetics This general category includes nylon, rayon, polyester, acrylic, and olefin. These fibers wear well and are naturally stain-resistant. Lower-quality fabrics may pill.

Natural Fibers Cotton, silk, wool, and linen can be woven alone or, for improved durability, blended with synthetics. Completely natural and natural-blend fabrics are less likely to pill than synthetics. Blends of natural fibers, particularly cotton and linen, are often used for upholstery. Leather and suede, two other natural fabrics, are extremely durable and are a great choice for upholstery in rooms that receive heavy use.

LEE

SUMMER

CHARLES

For less than the $1,000, this patio has become the primary entertaining area in the home. The majority of the budget was spent on fabric and accessories to make the space feel more like a well-decorated interior room. Prior to its makeover, *right*, the patio served primarily as a storage area for outdoor equipment.

BEFORE

PATIO LIVING

Fabric is a necessary ingredient for transforming a basic outdoor area into a cozy gathering space. Use it to weave together the various elements of your design scheme and to bring color and softness to outdoor furnishings and architecture.

Design Goal

This backyard patio served more as storage than living space. The owners longed for a space that was more comfortable and inviting.

Inside Out

To make your outdoor living space as welcoming as an indoor one, decorate it in the same way as you would an interior room, keeping in mind nature's elements. Prior to its makeover, this long, narrow backyard patio had all of the essential ingredients an outdoor gathering space requires—comfortable patio chairs, a gas grill, and a dining table. But the cool gray color scheme—created by gray-painted stucco and support posts, concrete flooring, and steel furnishings—and the awkward furniture arrangement were less than inviting. If this description sounds like your outdoor room, use these simple techniques to bring more comfort and color into your space.

Color Weave

Choose an outdoor color scheme as you would an indoor one. Consider colors that complement your home's exterior siding or trim, patio umbrella, awning, or even your garden flowers. For this patio makeover, accent colors in the chair cushions served as the catalyst for the color scheme.

If your patio has some interesting architectural detailing, such as an alcove or outdoor fireplace, set it off by painting it a contrasting color. To give the plain fireplace on this patio more prominence, the *Design on a Dime* crew painted the surrounding facade wall a golden yellow.

Six Steps to Design Success

1. Planning. Breaking up the long bowling-alley patio into three zones makes the space more functional and more inviting.
2. Color. Fabric panels, toss pillows, and a jute rug fill the lanai with color. A contrasting wall color sets off the fireplace alcove.
3. Furnishings. Existing pieces are rearranged to maximize comfort and to take advantage of the patio's best features, including the fireplace and the view of the pool.
4. Fabric. Canvas panels frame the lanai and warm the entire backyard.
5. Artwork and accessories. Potted plants bring in more color and life. Heavy, wind-resistant accessories also help make an outdoor space feel more inviting.
6. Lighting. A simple ceiling fan and light combine with wall sconces and firelight to give the area a warm glow at night.

Decorative ceramic tiles, mounted on plywood and framed, serve as weatherproof wall art. Lee purchased the tiles from a home center and mounted the piece high on the wall to protect it from the wind and to draw more attention to the fireplace area.

Outdoor Accessories

To give this old table *left* new life, Charles sanded and refinished it. A new wire rack keeps cooking utensils handy and organized.

Terra-cotta half pots *below left,* purchased for under $20 apiece, serve as wall sconces when equipped with battery-operated lamps. To make the half pots appear more decorative, Lee painted them with golden flowers that match the wall.

Shade-loving potted plants *below* fill once empty corners with color and life and suit the temperate climate. Weather-resistant accessories and fabrics create an indoor feel.

Custom-made redwood storage boxes, *opposite,* keep pool toys and outdoor game gear handy, yet under wraps. The boxes double as seating when the family entertains a crowd.

Textile Transformation

Use all-weather fabrics generously. Here Summer designed and stitched curtainlike canvas panels to disguise the unappealing support posts of the lanai and to frame the view of the adjacent pool and garden. Matching canvas pillows tossed onto the patio chairs create a visual connection between the deep red panels and the patio chairs. A waterproof area rug brings softness to the dining area. You can also use fabric to cover tabletops, awnings, and seat cushions, and to make panels for shading the sun.

Easy Arrangements

Arrange furnishings to accommodate tasks and entertaining. Here the design team divided the porch into three functional areas—one for cooking, one for dining, and one for lounging—and then arranged the furnishings to accommodate each task.

To make cooking and dining outdoors more comfortable, Summer recommends keeping grilling utensils handy by either hanging them near the grill or storing them in a rolling cart. A table placed near the grill is also convenient for holding spices, marinades, and serving platters.

For dining, choose comfortable chairs that encourage guests to linger long after the last course is served. For lounging, consider adding footstools and chaises that encourage relaxation.

Dressed for Success

To be a well-dressed room, an outdoor living space also requires the same finishing touches as an indoor room. Use under-eaves space to display weather-resistant artwork like the pottery sconces and the framed ceramic tiles *opposite bottom right*. Items made from wire, redwood, and powder-coated metals also work well. Be sure to choose pieces that are sturdy enough to withstand a swift breeze. Fill empty corners with potted plants and side tables, and then introduce accessories such as birdhouses, rocks, fountains, gazing balls, and decorative watering cans. Shelves are great for displaying potted arrangements and architectural salvage.

Project Costs

Refinishing the table: $16
Ceiling fan and light: $50
Pottery and plants: $306
Jute rug: $106
Canvas cabana curtains: $170
Tiled wall plaque: $81
Towel storage pot: $28
Redwood storage boxes: $200
Total cost: $957

Withstanding the Weather

Unless you plan to store your outdoor fabric-covered items during inclement weather, you'll need to choose fabrics and cushion fillings that can withstand moisture and sunlight. For open, unprotected patios choose a synthetic fabric rated for all-weather use. All-weather acrylic is an excellent choice because it is mildew-resistant and can withstand 1,000 sunlight hours without fading. Similarly, all-weather polyester vinyl repels moisture and resists mildew and can withstand 500 hours in the sun. For cushion filling, look for mildew- and moisture-resistant fills that dry quickly.

In protected areas, such as on a three-season porch, sturdy natural fibers such as treated canvas make viable covering options, but for increased longevity, you'll want to bring these items in during rainy periods.

Outdoor Comfort

Once lined up against the home's exterior wall, the furniture *opposite* is now grouped into zones for conversation (in front of the fireplace) and for dining. The face-to-face arrangement of chairs anchored by the fireplace mimics the way you would arrange furniture indoors in the living room. A waterproof area rug defines the eating area and helps to break up the long bowling-alley effect of the patio.

A large decorative urn *above* holds towels for guests and fills a once-empty corner. The terra-cotta tones complement the new color scheme.

For more great outdoor decorating ideas and inspiration, visit <u>HGTV.com/patios</u>.

Look for outdoor-rated electric spotlights, chandeliers, and sconces at lighting stores and home centers. For this space, the design team chose a powerful ceiling fan with a light kit and paired it with existing electric sconces and new candlelit ones.

Eyelet and Grommet Kits

These little metal or plastic rings provide a quick and affordable way to attach hooks or cords to drapery panels, awnings, shower curtains, or any type of fabric panel or decorative paper. Kits include everything you need to punch the hole into the fabric and to attach the ring (which reinforces the hole), as well as several dozen of the fastening rings themselves. For fail-safe results, look for kits that include a quality hole punch, a grommet or eyelet setting tool, and an anvil.

DRESS UP PORCH PILLARS

Bring instant color and softness to hard structural supports with a fabric cover-up. Choose acrylic fabrics designed for outdoor use.

Step-By-Step:

1. From the solid color fabric, cut a panel 4 inches longer than the pillar's height and 8 inches wider than the pillar's width.

2. From the patterned fabric, cut two border strips 4 inches longer than the pillar's height and 13 inches wide. Cut a 13-inch-wide border strip for the hem the width of the solid-color panel plus 25 inches. For the tieback strip, cut a 9×20-inch rectangle.

3. On the right side of each panel, reinforce the top edge with a strip of iron-on interfacing.

4. With right sides facing and raw edges aligned, stitch the side border strips to the long edges of one panel, using ½-inch seams. On the long raw edge of each border strip, turn under 1 inch twice and stitch close to the second fold.

5. With right sides facing and raw edges aligned, stitch the bottom border strip to the bottom edge of the panel. Hem the bottom border by turning under 1 inch twice and stitching close to the second fold.

6. At the top edge of the panel, turn under 1 inch twice and stitch close to the second fold. Repeat steps 1–6 to make the second panel for the pair that will wrap one pillar.

7. Sew the hook side of a strip of hook-and-loop tape to the inside edge of each border strip on one panel. Stitch the loop side to the corresponding edges on the remaining panel.

8. Using a grommet kit, install five evenly spaced grommet rings along the reinforced top edge of the panels (photo A).

9. Install the cup hooks in the fascia board on each side of the pillar. Install the first two close to the edges of the fascia board and the third in the center. Slip the grommets over the cup hooks (photo B).

10. Secure the panels around the poles by pressing the hook-and-loop tape together.

11. To make the tiebacks, fold each strip in half lengthwise with right sides facing. Stitch ends and sides, leaving an opening along the side. Clip corners, turn right side out, and slip-stitch the opening closed. Sew hook-and-loop tape to the ends. Wrap the tieback around the curtains (photo C).

You Will Need

- Solid-color all-weather fabric
- Complementary patterned all-weather fabric
- Scissors
- Iron-on interfacing strips
- Hook-and-loop fastening tape
- Matching thread
- Sewing needle or sewing machine
- Pins
- Grommet kit—5 grommets per panel (see Eyelet and Grommet kits on *page 118*)
- Cup hooks (about 6 per pillar)

Before the makeover, this master suite *right* felt unfinished. Now the room serves as an everyday getaway that encourages relaxation and togetherness.

BEFORE

FABRIC FINESSE

Bring a fresh look to a stale bedroom with tactile fabrics in alluring colors. Paired with easy-care, budget-conscious weaves, exotic textiles bring panache to bed coverings, canopies, toss pillows, folding screens, and even artwork.

Design Goal

The owners of this master bedroom wanted to transform their basic bedroom into an alluring tropical retreat.

Inspiration Point

One of the easiest ways to enliven an unadorned bedroom is through the addition of color and texture via accent pillows, bed linens, and either a fabric-covered headboard or canopy. For this suite, the owners wanted the room to feel like an island getaway, and imported fabrics provided an easy way to create an enticing and exotic ambience.

The striped toss pillow fabric *opposite* was the starting point for the suite's color scheme. A swatch of colorful fabric offers an easy way to choose a color scheme, Summer says. If the colors look great together on the fabric, they will also look great together in a room. Here one stripe color from the pillow suggests the sienna wall color, another stripe color defines the shade of burgundy for the bedding, and still another stripe color sets the tone for woven rattan furnishings and other decorative accents. Because the fabric pattern on the pillow is somewhat bold, Summer chose a small, repeat print sari fabric (see Sari Fabrics *right*) for the bedspread and the canopy. To reduce fabric costs, Summer limited the silk sari fabric to a wide stripe down the center of the comforter and repeated the same design on the canopy. A plain white cotton fabric frames the luxurious silk and skirts the bed as well. A matching cotton-covered folding screen hides a treadmill in one corner of the room.

Six Steps to Design Success

1. Planning. Lee, Charles, and Summer transformed a blasé bedroom into a cozy, tropical paradise with sumptuous fabrics.
2. Color. Vibrant sienna-color walls envelope the room in warmth and complement the wood floors and existing wood blinds.
3. Furnishings. A custom-made canopy replaces an out-of-place sleigh bed and makes the bed into a focal point. Two rattan chairs and a simple tray table affordably furnish a seating nook.
4. Fabric. Sari fabric adorns the bed's comforter and canopy. Complementary fabrics cover decorative accent pillows.
5. Artwork and accessories. Live plants combine with framed art to fill empty wall and floor space.
6. Lighting. Low-cost table lamps provide practical task and mood lighting.

Sari Fabrics

Sari fabric, a fabric that women from India and Pakistan commonly use to make robe-like dresses, is available at larger fabric retail stores and online. The elegant silk, linen, and pima cotton fabrics often feature rich, beautiful colors and metallic threads and can bring an exotic touch to furnishings and accessories.

Finishing Flourishes

Lee made these palm print cutouts *above* using a jigsaw, and then he framed them with picture frame molding purchased from a home center.

To give this surfing poster *above right* a more finished appearance, Charles made a frame from decorative molding and then stained it to match other woodwork in the room.

Transform a basic bed into a focal point with updated bed linens and a matching canopy *right*. For instructions on how to make a canopy like this one, see page 125.

Give your mantel an instant makeover by leaning a large framed mirror on the mantel shelf and flanking it with tall candlesticks *opposite*. For more design flair, you could layer a framed print in front of the mirror.

Art Connection

Once you have your colors defined and your bedding fabric chosen, look for artwork and accessories that reinforce your scheme. If your room has a fireplace, make the mantel a focal point by topping it with large-scale artwork and accessories. Although the marble fireplace in this suite was sleek and attractive, it lacked a mantel shelf. As a solution, Charles made a simple wooden shelf from a piece of solid mahogany and then stained the wood to match the floor. A new mirror, featuring a woven rattan pattern on the frame, reflects the vibrant wall color. A single candlestick and a glass vase filled with dried eucalyptus define a new focal point for the suite.

Choose artwork for your bedroom walls that further conveys your overall theme. You can make affordable artwork by framing found objects such as pictures from a colorful calendar, black and white photos or postcards, or even abstract-print fabrics. To create new artwork with a tropical flair, Lee used a jigsaw to cut out the shapes of palm fronds from two pieces of plywood. He then made frames from stock molding. An existing poster of surfers riding the waves also received a new frame.

Sitting Room

For bedroom seating, choose pieces that suit your design in terms of size, color, and functionality. Prior to its makeover, the overstuffed chair in this room seemed too large for the space, and it did not provide adequate seating for two. To solve the problem, the *Design on a Dime* team purchased two inexpensive rattan chairs and then softened their look with accent pillows. For another easy seating solution, consider slipcovering existing furnishings to complement your design.

Lamplight

Table and floor lamps are excellent sources for task lighting in the bedroom. To provide comfortable spots for reading in this suite, the design team placed lamps on each side of the bed and between the two new rattan chairs. Carefully placed candles provide additional mood lighting.

Project Costs
Paint and supplies: $58
New furniture: bed frame, canopy frame, rattan chairs, and folding screen: $168
New mantel and accessories: $275
Fabric for canopy, bedding, pillows, and screen: $225
Framing materials and plywood cutouts: $79
Lamps: $125
Potted plants: $70
Total Cost: $1,000

outdoor feel

Give your indoor spaces a tropical ambience with potted plants and rattan and bamboo furnishings. For more advice on plantscaping, see page 138. Dark-color wood furnishings and crisp white accents suggest the flavor of British West Indies style.

Make a plain comforter look custom-made by sewing a strip of designer fabric down the center as shown.

MAKE A BAMBOO CANOPY

Make a canopy similar to this in an afternoon. For more ideas on making custom headboards, including video demonstrations, visit HGTV.com/headboards.

You Will Need

Two complementary fabrics, one solid, one patterned

Matching thread

Sewing machine

Five bamboo poles: three cut 3 inches longer than the width of bed; two cut 50 inches

Epoxy glue

Drill with screw bit

Wood screws

Sisal rope

4 plant hanger hooks

Stud finder

Step-By-Step

1. From solid fabric, cut two border strips 12 inches wide and 90 inches long for the headboard panel; two border strips 12 inches wide and 32 inches long for the drape; and two top panels the width of the bed by 48 inches.

2. From the patterned fabric cut a panel 90 inches long and 20 inches narrower than the width of the bed. Cut a second panel 32 inches long and 20 inches narrower than the bed width.

3. Stitch the 90-inch-long border strips to the 90-inch-long patterned panel, using a ½-inch seam allowance. Stitch the 32-inch-long border strips to the 32-inch-long patterned panel.

4. Stitch the two top panels together, right sides facing, leaving an opening for turning. Turn to the right side; press; slip-stitch the opening closed.

5. Hem the sides and one end of the headboard and drape panels by turning under 1 inch twice and stitching close to the second fold. Join the panels to the canopy top.

6. For the canopy frame, cut the poles to size (photo A).

7. Lay the bamboo poles on a flat surface to form a rectangle, resting the long poles atop the short ones. Position the remaining bamboo pole across the center of the rectangle. Use epoxy glue to join the bamboo. After the glue sets, turn the frame over and reinforce the corners with screws (photo B).

8. Cover the points of joining with sisal rope, wrapping in an X pattern around the poles.

9. With a stud finder, locate ceiling studs near the points where the canopy corners will hang. Attach plant hooks to the ceiling studs.

10. Attach the canopy to the plant hooks with equal lengths of sisal rope (photo C).

TIP: For quicker construction, use a flat bedsheet as your canopy fabric.

"Deep, tropical colors and imported fabrics create a cozy, exotic feel." – Summer Baltzer

A floral area rug anchors the seating arrangement and divides the large room into more intimate areas. Ready-made curtain panels, purchased from a discount store, soften the window casings without blocking too much light.

BEFORE

OUTSIDE IN

As illustrated on pages 112–119, you can make an outdoor space feel like a well-dressed interior by introducing the right mix of fabrics and accessories. Here the design plan is just the opposite—to bring the pleasure of a cottage garden inside the home.

Design Goal

A young family longed to give their cavernous and dated living room an inviting, fresh-air ambience.

Garden Style

The pleasure of garden style is that no matter where you live or what the season, you can enjoy an alfresco feel. Soft colors and vintage botanical patterns are key elements of the design, as are garden accessories and timeworn furnishings. White is a staple of this decorating scheme—use it generously on furnishings and accessories. Pair it with pastel shades of green, used as a backdrop here, and then add accent colors inspired by your own garden. The soft lavenders and faded berry colors sprinkled throughout this living area can be seen in the backyard view.

Ready-made slipcovers provide an easy way to lighten dark or dated upholstery while giving a summery outdoor feel. Bring color and comfort to slipcovered furnishings with tactile chenille throws and down-stuffed toss pillows.

Breezy Fabrics

Faded, vintage-look look fabrics in a variety of patterns cover the plethora of toss pillows on this sofa and love seat. Stripes, florals, and plaids of varying scales achieve pattern harmony via similar color combinations. The same colors repeat on the area rug, helping to create a cohesive feel. When looking for fabrics to complement your decorating scheme, do what Kristan does—choose fabrics that have two or three common accent colors, but with varying degrees of dominance. For example, the striped fabric on the toss pillows *opposite* has more green than berry, while the berry dominates the floral motif. Both feature the same creamy white background that matches the slipcovers.

Six Steps to Design Success

1. Planning. Erasing the line between indoors and outdoors makes this interior space feel as cozy as a secret garden.
2. Color. Soft sage green serves a backdrop for lush berries and soft lavenders.
3. Furnishings. Slipcovers give worn furnishings a fresh, new look. New pieces, painted and distressed to look old, bring in vintage warmth.
4. Fabric. Botanical prints on the rug and toss pillows define the overall color scheme and fill the room with garden flavor.
5. Artwork and accessories. Live plants combine with architectural salvage and everyday items to fill walls and display spaces attractively and affordably.
6. Lighting. Low-cost floor lamps combine with a bargain-priced chandelier (wired to a dimmer switch) to provide ambient and accent lighting.

Shelf and mantel kits provide an easy way to bring dimension to flat walls. Change the displays frequently to show off favorite photos and mementos.

Pulling it Together

When entertaining guests, splurge on a few extras, such as these white roses *left*.

Dave made this table *below left* from finish-grade plywood and precarved legs. To finish the table as Dave did, prime, then paint the assembled piece with a brown base coat and allow the paint to dry. Top with two coats of a paler color, such as the soft sage green used here, and allow the paint to dry thoroughly. Use medium- and fine-grain sandpaper to sand off the painted finish on tabletop edges and legs to resemble wear.

This darkly stained table *below*, purchased from a discount store, adds a touch of contrast and helps create a casual, evolved-over-time look.

Fanciful Furnishings

To furnish a garden room, fill it as you would an outdoor escape, with comfortably weathered tables and garden rockers woven together with painted color. Choose pieces with classic period details, such as turned legs and carved corbels. Custom-made by Dave, the coffee table *opposite bottom left* features artfully carved legs and a distressed two-tone paint finish.

Fresh Air Accents

Urns, topiaries, and terra-cotta pots underscore a garden scheme, as do everyday objects displayed as fine art. If you love old iron gates or picket fences, display them on the wall. Salvaged window frames *right* fill the wall behind the love seat with simple pattern.

Use large-scale whitewashed baskets to corral magazines and books and to display fresh or silk floral arrangements. Top tables with vintage-look platters, old-fashioned milk pitchers, and pairs of candlesticks. To make a tiled platter like the one *opposite top left,* see page 131.

Romantic Lighting

When planning a lighting scheme for a garden room, think sunshine. Leave windows entirely bare or top them with a simple valance. Rustic shutters also complement a garden look—but if you go this route, you'll want to choose a style that can be opened fully to let in as much sunshine as possible. If privacy is an issue, choose simple white, light-filtering panels like the semisheer linen curtains *opposite below right.*

Garden-style chandeliers, such as the vintage fixture shown on page 126, provide beautiful ambient light, while shaded lamps create a warm evening glow. For more romance, top tables with vintage candelabras or a platter filled with pillar candles.

Project Costs

Fabric and window treatments: $279
Art and accessories: $342
Furniture: $212
Lighting: $139
Paint and supplies: $21
Total Cost: $993

Everyday items make attractive wall art. These old-fashion lace-edged plates hang from ribbons threaded through the existing cutouts. The teardrop shape created by the hanging plates lends symmetry and balance to the display.

This chair was pulled from a nearby room and refinished to match the new decor. A new fabric on the chair seat matches one of the toss pillows. The occasional table was purchased from a thrift store and painted to match the chair.

TILE A TRAY

Make an old tray look like a family heirloom by covering it with broken tiles.

Step-By-Step

1. Arrange the ceramic pieces on the inside of the tray, adjusting them as necessary to create a pleasing arrangement (photo A).

2. Remove the tiles from the tray one at a time, arranging them on the work surface in the same pattern as on the tray.

3. Apply epoxy to the back of each tile with the paintbrush and press it in place on the tray bottom.

4. Allow the adhesive to set according to the manufacturer's instructions.

5. Line the inside edge of the tray with painter's tape to protect the sides from the grout. Mix the grout according to the manufacturer's instructions, and pour it over the tiles (photo B). With a clean, damp sponge, spread the grout over the tiles, pushing it into all of the crevices between the tile pieces (photo C).

6. Wipe excess grout off the surface of the tiles with a clean, damp sponge. Let the grout dry slightly, and then wipe away any remaining powdery glaze.

7. Let the grout cure as directed by manufacturer. Remove the blue painter's tape.

You Will Need

- Old serving tray with sides that are at least 1 inch tall
- Broken tile pieces or mosaic tiles
- Super-strength epoxy
- Old household paintbrush
- Painter's tape
- Grout
- Clean, damp sponge

"The charm of the garden is yours year-round when you decorate with garden style."
— Kristan Cunningham

Fresh fruits look great atop a dining table, especially when they are displayed in unusual ways, such as inside tall glass canisters or vases.

STEP

5

ACCESSORIZING YOUR ROOM

When combined with existing furnishings, accessories and accents make a room feel complete.

ACCESSORIZING YOUR ROOM

Like fabulous shoes to a snazzy outfit, art and accessories make a room pop.

Wall Decor

The walls inside your home form a backdrop for daily living and provide you with a canvas for personal expression. To make them as inviting as the other components in your room, choose a well-balanced mix of color, texture, and scale.

In every room, one wall inevitably draws the eye more than the others. This focal-point wall may be home to a dominant feature, such as a fireplace, built-ins, or a wall of windows. In other rooms, however, the wall that draws your eye may be a nondescript surface that stands behind a major piece of furniture, such as a sofa, dining table, or bed. Left empty or haphazardly decorated with undersize elements, these walls make a room feel sterile and incomplete. To avoid this, do as the *Design on a Dime* design coordinators do in many homes: Use lackluster walls as an opportunity to personalize a room with colorful, interesting artwork, dinnerware, and more.

More Than a Pretty Picture

If you think the only item you can hang on a wall is a framed picture, think again. There is an array of wall art to choose from, including plates and platters, textiles, wall vases, baskets, hats, clocks, architectural salvage pieces, and decorative sconces. When shopping for wall art, look at things not for what they are, but for what they could be. A shiny silver platter looks lovely when displayed on a wall next to silver-plate picture frames and silver sconces. Architectural salvage, such as weathered window mullions, paired with small prints in distressed frames or a black wrought-iron gate and matching black sconces, also make artistic wall displays.

Wall art helps define and anchor a space. Here, a combination of shelves and a tile mosaic turn the breakfast area into a focal point.

Framed tile mosaics combine with home center shelves and an existing sconce to create a composition that's both aesthetically pleasing and functional *above*.

Wall Art Priorities

To help you decide what new pieces of wall art will have the most impact on your decor, ask yourself these questions:

• Which wall in this room does everybody look at when they first enter?

• If money weren't a factor, what would you like to see on this wall? Can you create a similar, less expensive version by framing a print or hiring an amateur artist, such as a college student, to paint an original work designed to fit this spot?

• Do you like what's on your walls now? If so, what could you add that would draw more attention to your favorite work or create better balance with the surrounding furnishings?

• Is the wall you are planning to decorate exposed to direct sunlight? If so, you'll want to avoid hanging vintage textiles, such as old quilts and tapestries, or any original art or costly reproductions in this spot. Instead, choose something that can be easily replaced should the sun fade the colors or weaken the fibers.

As you narrow your art selections, consider the style and mood you've defined through the color, furnishing, and fabric selections you've already made, then choose items that complement the ambience that is unfolding. Remember that you'll need to add some kind of wall hanger to the pieces you choose; if the items are heavy, securely attach them to a wall stud.

Scale and Proportion

Your first purchases—and the first pieces you hang—should be the largest and boldest decorations, or a grouping of several smaller items hung together for impact. Proportion and scale are critical: A large oil painting may look overbearing over a small, spindly chair, while a tiny framed photo may appear lost on an otherwise empty wall. To ensure eye-pleasing relationships between artwork and furnishings, balance the two in a ratio of 3:4. For example, the framed mirrors and sconces on page 142 are about three-fourths the width of the console table below.

Once you complete the arrangement on your focal point wall, turn your attention to the surrounding vertical planes, again keeping in mind scale and proportion. These side walls should be decorated to look just as as enticing but on a smaller scale than the focal point wall. Rooms that have too many focal points can seem uncomfortably busy and cluttered, with too many areas competing for attention. There should be a few intentionally empty areas on each wall where the eye can rest.

"When displaying your collections, keep in mind that grouping related items gives them greater impact than scattering like items around the room."
—Summer Baltzer

ACCESSORY SHOPPING WORKSHEET *Wall Art and Accent Pieces*

Materials to Purchase	Quantity	Cost Per Unit	Total Cost (Qty x Unit Cost)	Source/Store	Comments
Architectural Salvage					
Clocks					
Decorative Sconces					
Decorative Shelving					
Dimensional Art					
Framed Paintings					
Framed Prints					
Hanging Baskets					
Hats					
Plates and Platters					
Tapestries					
Wall-Hung Quilts					
Wall-Hung Vases					
Other					

Put rarely used serving pieces to work as floral holders or accent pieces. This silver-plate coffeepot makes an elegant vase for fresh flowers.

The Right Frame
The best frames enhance rather than overwhelm what they frame. Choose a frame that provides enough contrast to make the imagery or mirror stand out from the wall while harmonizing with the art. This balance of contrast and harmony ensures a positive decorating impact.

Tabletop Accessories

Carefully chosen accessories make each room in your home one of a kind and provide everyone who enters a glimpse of the personalities of the people who reside there. As with wall art, these accessories need to be displayed in focal-point areas while keeping proportion and balance in mind. As a general rule, bigger is usually better. A pair of tall candlesticks anchored by a chubby vase has more visual impact than a trio of small figurines. If you have a collection of miniature ceramics or teacups, display them in shadow boxes hung on the wall or layered on a mantel or shelf instead of individually.

One trick to creating interesting, well-balanced displays is to love what you display—but don't display everything you love. Edit your displays for impact and leave a few surfaces open to separate high-impact areas. To create visual continuity, group objects by shape, color, texture, or material. Wherever you can, tell a story with each display: Grouped together, certain objects can tell a narrative of your life—from where you've traveled to whom you cherish the most.

Plantscaping

Flowers and greenery bring life to a room. Whether you prefer fresh-cut, silk, or dried flowers or live potted plants, choose arrangements that complement the overall attitude of your room. With the right greenery and floral arrangements, you can enhance the ambience of a room by drawing attention to favorite furnishings, artwork, and accessories, and if necessary, disguising awkward structural supports or dark, unwelcoming corners. As with other accessories, bigger is usually better. Fill an empty corner in the dining room by displaying a large fern on a pretty plant stand. Set off a window wall by nestling a ficus tree next to it, or add life to a coffee table with a colorful arrangement of fresh flowers. If you find yourself the owner of three or four smaller plants, group them together and display them on a corner of a snack bar or on tiered tables in the corner of a bedroom, along with a couple of floor-size plants.

SHOP SMART WORKSHEET *Accent Pieces*

Materials to Purchase	Quantity	Cost Per Unit	Total Cost (Qty x Unit Cost)	Source/Store	Comments
Candelabras					
Candleholders					
Candles					
Floral Arrangements					
Green Plants					
Photo Frames					
Sculptures					
Vases					
Other					

"Whether they're alike or charmingly dissimilar, objects in odd-numbered groupings create symmetry that's pleasing to the eye."
— Spencer Anderson

KRISTAN

SPENCER

DAVE

Accessories, such as table runners, area rugs, and fresh fruit and flowers, make guests feel instantly welcome. Before its makeover, this room *right* did little to encourage guests to linger and relax.

BEFORE

FINISHING TOUCHES

If you have a room that functions well but feels uninviting, the only thing missing may be a few finishing touches. The Before and After shots of this dining room show how artwork and accessories can take a room from bland to beautiful.

Design Goal

The owners of this bare-bones, but functional, eating area requested a room with enough design dash to entice family and friends to gather in the space every day.

Artful Plan

The room where your family and friends gather to dine and enjoy conversation should emanate hospitality. To nurture that welcoming feeling, you'll need more than just a nice dining set. Accessory furnishings, fabrics, wall color, artwork, tabletop displays, and lighting should all coordinate to make the room feel as inviting as possible.

Furniture Finish

Critique your current dining room arrangement. Would you open up more floor space if you placed your table at an angle to the walls? Would the table fit the space better if it were turned 180 degrees? What fills the corners of the room? Is there a spot for a cozy club chair or rocker, or even a side table and lamp or a plant stand? By rearranging the furnishings in this dining room, designers Kristan, Spencer, and Dave opened up enough floor space for a console table, two round occasional tables, and a long wooden bench. Spencer made the console table and then gave it a crackle finish to imbue a sense of age. The unfinished three-leg occasional tables, purchased from a discount department store, are kept undercover by white, round 60-inch tablecloths. Dave found the 1930s-era

Six Steps to Design Success

1. Planning. The black furniture and white woodwork provided the design spark for this scheme.
2. Color. Pale green walls add personality.
3. Furnishings. A few smaller pieces add comfort and style and fill the voids in the original design.
4. Fabric. A table runner, toss pillows, and new curtain panels soften the look of the room.
5. **Artwork. Decorative plates, mirrors, and sconces help fill empty walls. More items can be added over time.**
6. Lighting. Table lamps and candles enhance the light from the existing chandelier.

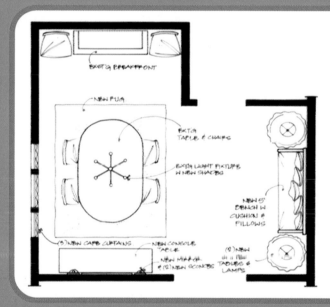

The new furniture arrangement makes the most of the L-shape space, with the long leg of the L dedicated to dining. Extra seating fills the short leg.

Dressed for Dinner

Fabric left over from the cushions trims the cafe curtains *above* and connects windows to furnishings. For more design dash, make napkins or a table runner from the same fabric as the curtain panels.

Vintage sterling silver pieces *above right* are family heirlooms and provide extra sparkle when grouped below an oval mirror and mirror-backed sconces.

Give a wrought-iron wall sconce *right* more importance and sparkle by hanging it over a beveled-edge mirror. Wire on crystals and glue a crystal candlestick to the sconce's candleholder to complete the transformation.

On the table *opposite,* fresh fruits and flowers are tabletop staples. Here green apples stack in tall glass vases and gerbera daisies emerge from a silver coffeepot.

bench at an antiques shop and painted it black to match the existing furnishings. Kristan topped the bench with a thick seat cushion and a multitude of toss pillows made from black and white geometric prints and red and green floral fabrics. The pillow colors bring out the subtle accents in the new, primarily black and white floral area rug, which now anchors the dining table. All these "accessory" furnishings fill up empty space and make the large room feel cozy.

Winsome Walls

Because guests in this room spend a great deal of time seated, it is the perfect place to display cherished wall art. To ensure a pleasing placement, sit at each chair around the table and look at your current wall displays. Are the pictures hanging at the appropriate height to be viewed from a seated position? Do the groupings appear balanced and coordinated? Does the wall color complement the artwork? Would a contrasting or coordinating paint color help make your displays more visually appealing?

Before the *Design on a Dime* makeover, the plain white walls in this room felt cold and uninviting and wall decor was nonexistent. Today a wash of celery green paint coats the walls in color and helps make the new black and white accessories pop.

Eye-Catching Art

Kristan chose black and white accents to tie the existing 1930s-style black-painted hutch and chairs with the existing white woodwork. Cottage-style black and white plates, black and white candle sconces, and a black framed oval mirror bring color, pattern, and shine to the once-empty walls. Divided into two displays, each new wall vignette is arranged in a symmetrical, balanced pattern.

Project Costs

Paint and supplies: $55
Furniture: $344
Artwork and accessories: $153
Lighting: $164
Area rug: $150
Textiles: $130
Total Cost: $996

Fabric Flourishes

Simple cafe curtains, made by combining a black and white striped remnant with a tone-on-tone semi-transparent cotton, soften the lines of the window and help make the window wall as attractive as the other three. Shutters hanging inside the room make the window appear larger than its actual dimensions.

Light Touch

To soften the ambient light from the chandelier, Kristan purchased lampshades to cover each bulb. For romantic meals, a pair of candle sconces and pillar candles can be lit. If necessary, this candlelight can be supplemented with light from a pair of new table lamps flanking the bench.

Coordinate fabric wall hangings, window treatments, rugs, and upholstery. The colors for these fabrics were defined by the area rug shown on page 140.

Custom Looks, Do-It-Yourself Price

Adding designer details to items you make yourself lends a sophisticated touch that will make your guests think you are an artist—or that you hired one. For example, Kristan gave the bench cushion *above* and *opposite below* extra pizzazz by using a striped fabric on the cushion's edges and a floral fabric on the cushion's top.

The W monogram on the center toss pillow took just minutes to paint and creates a personal style statement. Additional toss pillows are made from the same fabric as the cushion's accent stripe, as well as a red and cream floral that introduces a lively accent color.

Practical Beauty

Cloth-covered side tables *above* affordably fill the dining area's empty corners and provide a perfect spot for table lamps. Because this dining area also serves as a passageway between the kitchen and living room, the owners use these lamps nearly every night.

When shopping for a dining room chandelier, *above right*, look for a style that harmonizes with the rest of the room's furnishings. For added light control, attach the fixture to a dimmer switch.

The decorative W on the largest pillow *right* was created using a fabric paint marker. Kristan drew on the letter freehand, but if you have less faith in your lettering abilities, you could use a stencil.

APPLY A CRACKLE FINISH

Add texture and interest to plain wood furniture with a contrasting crackle finish.

Step-By-Step

1. Lightly sand all surfaces to be painted; remove dust with a tack cloth.

2. Apply the base coat to the entire piece, using a paintbrush. Let the base coat dry thoroughly.

3. Following the manufacturer's directions, apply the crackle medium to all surfaces (photo A). Allow the medium to cure for the recommended length of time.

4. For cracks that follow the wood grain, brush on the top coat with a paintbrush, consistently brushing in one direction (photo B). Do not overlap brush strokes because this will interfere with the crackling. For more random, veinlike cracks, dab on the top coat with a sea sponge, being careful not to sponge over already sponged areas. Let the top coat dry.

5. Apply two or three coats of water-base polyurethane, allowing the polyurethane to dry between coats.

You Will Need

Console table or other wood furnishing
Sandpaper, tack cloth
Creamy white (or desired color) flat or eggshell latex paint for base coat
Crackle medium
Black (or desired color) flat or eggshell latex paint for top coat
Paintbrushes, paint tray
Optional: Sea sponge
Optional: Water-base polyurethane

> *"Make a new piece of furniture look ages old with a crackle-finish paint treatment."*
> — Dave Sheinkopf

Dress your dining room windows to match the style of your furnishings and architecture. When combined with decorative shutters, these simple cafe curtains complement both the dining decor and the style of this 75-year-old home and still allow in plenty of daylight.

LEE

SUMMER

CHARLES

The bed quilt defined the color scheme for the room and gave the designers a sense of the resident's personal taste.

BEFORE

PERSONAL SPACE

More than a sleeping spot, your bedroom serves as a place where you can go to unwind, rejuvenate, and enjoy quiet conversation or solitude. Comfort comes first, followed by an array of pampering amenities.

Design Goal

The renter of this dark and lifeless apartment bedroom requested a room with a much more inviting and personal look.

Essential Amenities

To make your bedroom feel like a refuge from the rest of the world, start with a mattress that exudes comfort, then add the amenities that are essential to you and whomever you share the space with. If you love music, add a sound system. If you enjoy travel, set up a display of the keepsakes you've collected from previous trips. Make space to display the treasures that make you smile—family photos, favorite books, or even heirloom folk art. The more personal the space feels to you (and your mate), the more comforting a sanctuary it will be.

Before its *Design on a Dime* makeover, the only thing in this room that matched the resident's personality was the colorful bed quilt. Lee opted to use this quilt as the starting point for a new design scheme. Paint color, upholstery, and accessory colors were all pulled from this patchwork piece.

Golden Glow

To brighten the walls and give your room a cocoonlike ambience, choose a warm, saturated paint color, such as the golden yellow used on two of the walls of this room or the muted pink that was chosen for the fabric accents. If you want your retreat to feel more soothing, Summer recommends choosing a cool, pale wall color, such as sky blue or sea green.

Six Steps to Design Success

1. Planning. Rearranging the furniture gives basic bedroom furnishings a more contemporary look.
2. Color. A warm, saturated color scheme makes the room feel cozy and intimate.
3. Furnishings. Secondhand furnishings provide comfy seating.
4. Fabric. Upholstered doors soften the impact of the massive closet door.
5. Artwork and accessories. Open shelves provide display space for personal collections. Vintage wooden boxes double as three-dimensional art and storage organizers.
6. Lighting. Three table lamps combine with an overhead fixture to light the deep-color room.

The shelving unit and apothecary drawers give the flat surfaces a sense of dimension while creating a personal decorating statement.

Artistic Elements

New toss pillows *above* accentuate the room's new color scheme.

Covering closet doors with batting and fabric as shown *above right* softens the door's overall appearance and brings more color and texture to the room's vertical surfaces.

This two-tiered shelf *right* was custom-made by Lee and emphasizes the bed as a focal point of the room. Items on display are both functional and attractive.

Almost anything that can be attached to the wall can serve as art. Baskets, trays, quilts, framed postcards or greeting cards are all excellent, affordable choices. *Opposite,* vintage apothecary drawers make an enticing display and provide storage for jewelry, needles, thread, and other small items.

Cozy Seating

When arranging furniture, consider putting the bed in a less-predictable spot. In this bedroom, angling the bed against one corner of the room gives the box-shape room more interest and opens up enough floor space for some cozy chairs. By scouring local secondhand shops, the design team was able to afford two small chairs, one upholstered in the same pink as the accent pillows and a second upholstered in complementary gold tones. For another seating option, Charles recovered a worn ottoman with a tone-on-tone corduroy and placed it against the foot of the bed.

Door Art

To make plain closet doors look more attractive, consider covering them in fabric as Summer did to the doors *opposite top right*. This tone-on-tone corduroy print was also used to cover the ottoman and the bed pillows. First staple on a thin sheet of batting as close to the edge of the doors as possible. In this case, Summer stapled the batting three or four times along the edges of each recessed panel. Staple panels of fabric over the batting. A decorative ribbon, secured with hot glue, disguises the staples.

Focal Point Display

To make the head of your bed a showcase, make a new headboard and fill the wall above it with display shelves. For this bed, Charles made a headboard from salvaged staircase balusters and precut, decorative moldings that he screwed in place. Above the bed, a custom-made corner shelving unit designed by Lee provides display space for some of the resident's most-cherished keepsakes.

Project Costs

Paint and supplies: $65
Furniture: $478
Window treatments: $130
Artwork and accessories: $325
Total Cost: $998

accent lights

A room with dark color walls requires more light than a pale or white room, as dark colors absorb light and light colors reflect it. To remedy this, the designers added accent lamps to this space.

Curtain panels made from eyelet-edged sheets soften the vertical blinds without breaking the budget. These panels were made for about $30.

MAKE A BALUSTER HEADBOARD

Transform mismatched staircase balusters (you can purchase them for a few dollars a piece from a salvage yard) into a one-of-a-kind headboard. For a video demonstration of this project and more, visit HGTV.com/dod.

Step-By-Step

1. From the 1×3s cut two pieces the width of your bed and two pieces the length of the balusters. Set the pieces on the 1-inch edge and secure with all-purpose screws to form a rectangular frame.

2. Arrange the balusters inside the frame, spacing them evenly. Drill pilot holes through the 1×3 frame into the top and bottom of each baluster. Secure balusters with all-purpose screws.

3. From 2×4s, cut a piece to fit the top of the baluster frame and two pieces to encase the sides and extend as legs for the headboard. Attach these support pieces to the baluster frame with all-purpose screws. To secure the mattress, cut a 1×3 board the width of the mattress and secure it to the legs at the appropriate height.

4. Cover the frame with decorative molding pieces, securing with trim screws near the corner joints (photos A and B).

5. Glue square decorative wood embellishments over the corners to conceal the screws (photo C).

6. Prime and paint the headboard. Apply two coats of polyurethane if desired.

7. Secure the headboard to the bed frame using all-purpose screws.

> **"You can create a headboard from any combination of decorative moldings and embellishments."**
> – Charles Burbridge

You Will Need

- 1×3 boards (see instructions for lengths)
- Saw
- Balusters
- 1⅝" all-purpose screws
- Drill with screw bit
- 2×4 boards
- Fluted window or door trim
- Eight 1⅝" trimhead screws
- 4 square decorative wooden embellishments
- Wood glue
- Latex primer
- Latex paint, high gloss finish
- Household paintbrushes
- Latex polyurethane (optional)

A hip, modern dinette set and a wall display made from mosaic tiles and floating shelves turn this once-empty end of the kitchen into a sleek but comfortable spot for casual meals.

BEFORE

KITCHEN COUTURE

At the heart of every home, the kitchen deserves to be as well-dressed as any other gathering area. To make this working space look pulled together, fill it with comfort, color, and texture.

Design Goal

The owners of this sterile galley kitchen wanted the space to feel as warm and welcoming as an earthy, retro-style family room.

Appetizing Palette

Kitchens are typically known for their function rather than their style. Surfaces tend to be cold and hard, and colors are often limited to cabinet finish and countertop material. To make the utilitarian space feel as friendly as a family room, warm the walls with color and bring in lots of accessories to fill the space with personality.

For this kitchen, *Design on a Dime* team members Lee, Charles, and Summer chose a pale milk chocolate color for the walls and then painted the originally all-white cabinets a darker chocolate color. To add more contrast and texture to the built-ins, cabinetry inserts are adorned with a sea-grass wallcovering (see pages 158–159). To bring more color to the walls, Lee grouted and framed mosaic tiles and then attached the framed designs to the walls behind the stove and eating area.

Earthy Accessories

When accessorizing a kitchen, blend form and function wherever possible. Mix pretty, useful items—such as collectible pottery, colorful oil bottles, and ceramic canisters—with purely decorative objects that offer glimpses of your individual style. Sculpture, glass vases, and fresh-cut garden flowers and grasses are all good accessory choices for kitchen countertops. At *right* matching spice bottles add natural color and pattern to the countertop.

Six Steps to Design Success

1. Planning. Painting the walls and cabinets and adding tile and shelving to the walls fill this once-sterile room with texture and style.
2. Color. Mosaic tiles purchased in 12×12-inch squares defined the color palette for the entire room.
3. Furnishings. A new table and rolling island add comfort and function.
4. Fabric. A washable runner warms and protects the kitchen's wood floor.
5. **Artwork and accessories. The display behind the table serves as a focal point for the kitchen.**
6. Lighting. Existing downlights and wall sconces provide both task and mood lighting.

Countertop accessories are both attractive and functional and include a cookbook and spice bottles.

Creating a mosaic display takes less time then you think. These 1×1-inch tiles come in 12×12-inch sheets held together by a paper backing. Lee used tile adhesive to attach the sheets to particleboard, then filled the evenly spaced joints with tinted grout. He designed the mosaic display *left* to fit around ready-made shelves.

Bamboo shoots bring natural color and texture to the tabletop *below*. Woven chargers make the table look dressed for dinner all day long.

Shelf Sensation

Building a focal point display in a kitchen or breakfast room adds a touch of elegance to these functional spaces. Use these principles of display to create an eye-pleasing composition on your shelves:

• **Repetition.** To make your display appear cohesive, create a visual connection by choosing an odd number of items that are the same color or shape. Items grouped in threes or fives are the most visually appealing.

• **Variety.** Tall objects emphasize vertical movement and add excitement. Large, unusually shaped objects provide a focal point within the display.

• **Balance.** Place one visually heavy item at each end of the shelf. Objects gain visual weight if they are large, colorful, dark, patterned, or unusually shaped. If necessary, elevate smaller items on a stack of books or a decorative stand.

• **Layering.** Add depth and color by placing smaller vases or a candlestick in front of plates and platters.

Stylish Furnishings

When choosing kitchen furnishings, look for pieces with eye-catching shapes and touchable textures. Here Lee, Summer, and Charles chose a sleek, round retro-look table. Behind the table, solid-wood floating shelves fit into custom-made mosaic wall murals to show off ceramic vases and shapely serving pieces.

Tactile Textiles

As with any other gathering area in your home, warm the floors with nubby area rugs and soften seats with comfy cushions. Line baskets and top tables with colorful fabric. For the windows, opt for treatments that can withstand spatters, such as vinyl or aluminum shades or wood shutters. Wooden miniblinds control sunlight in this kitchen and are as practical as they are pretty. A natural jute rug layers over the wood floor.

Practical Art

Like window treatments, kitchen art should be durable, not delicate. The framed mosaics used here add color and texture to the walls, and they are easily washable. When adding wall art to your kitchen, choose prints protected by tempered glass, or hang items made from sturdy, washable materials such as metal, glazed clay, or urethane-coated wood.

Flexible Lighting

Light work surfaces with undercabinet lights, pendants, recessed spots, or overhead fixtures. To give the kitchen a warm glow when cooking duties are over, add wall sconces *opposite above left* and pillar candles. Candles in the kitchen can also be used to absorb cooking odors; light several before sautéing garlic or onion.

An inexpensive jute rug warms the kitchen floor and matches the sea-grass cabinetry inserts.

Project Costs

Paint and supplies: $65
Cabinet makeover: $120
Tile art and shelves: $140
Table and chairs: $230
Accessories: $136
Butcher block island: $200
Wood blinds and door curtain: $108
Total Cost: $999

kitchen wall color

If you like the finish on your cabinets, accent them by painting the surrounding walls a deeper color such as terra-cotta or raspberry.

Painting the cabinets chocolate brown and decorating the recessed panels with sea grass purchased from a wallpaper outlet store adds warmth and color to this once all-white space. Miniblinds control sunlight and are impervious to splashes from the sink below.

PAINT AND PAPER CABINETS

Renew tired cabinets with a colorful painted finish, and then add more texture and interest by decorating the recessed center panel with a wallcovering.

Step-By-Step

1. Remove the cabinet doors and drawers; also remove the knobs, pulls, and hinges. Lightly sand all surfaces (or use a deglossing primer).

2. Prime all surfaces; let dry. (If you prefer a smoother finish, use a small foam roller instead of a brush.) Lightly sand the primed surfaces and wipe with a tack cloth.

3. Using low-tack painter's tape, mask off any areas that you don't want to paint, such as the center panel of a door that you plan to cover with grass cloth.

4. Paint the remaining surfaces with two coats of the base coat color, letting each coat dry thoroughly (see photo A).

5. Using a crafts knife and metal ruler, cut the wallcovering in rectangles to match the size of each inset center panel. If the wallcovering has a pattern, make sure your cutouts complement the pattern.

6. Following the manufacturer's instructions, use a foam brush to apply vinyl adhesive to the back of the wallcovering cutout (see photo B); "book" the wallcovering (fold it in half, adhesive sides facing) to set the adhesive.

7. Apply vinyl-to-vinyl adhesive to the cabinet door inset. Allow adhesive to set for the recommended time.

8. Smooth the cutout to the door inset, pressing it firmly with your hands (see photo C). With a crafts knife, score the wallcovering around the curved ends of the inset panels (see photo D). Use scissors to trim away the excess wallcovering.

9. Repeat steps 5 and 6 to cover the remaining panels. Let the wallcovering adhesive dry completely.

10. Reassemble the cabinets.

You Will Need

Screwdriver
Fine-grit sandpaper
Tack cloth
Latex primer
Latex paint, in dark chocolate or the color of your choice
Household paintbrush or small foam roller
Low-tack painter's tape
Foam brush (for applying wallpaper adhesive)
Sea-grass wallcovering or wallcovering of your choice
Crafts knife
Vinyl-to-vinyl wallpaper adhesive
Scissors

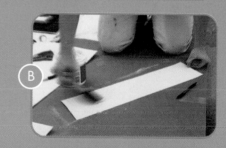

"Sea-grass wallpaper adds wonderful texture and is durable enough to use in the kitchen." — Summer Baltzer

Light color shades and blinds reflect more natural light than dark color ones. Choose them to cover the glass panes and reserve the more dramatic colors for valances and decorative side panels.

STEP

6

THE RIGHT LIGHT

THE RIGHT LIGHT

Whether you are writing a novel in your home office, creating a quiche in your kitchen, or watching a soap on the TV in the family room, the right light will make performing these activities more comfortable.

Overall Lighting

Also called ambient or general lighting, this light mimics natural light and enables you to see from one side of the room to the other. You can create this basic form of light from overhead fixtures, such as a large chandelier as shown *opposite* or with rows of track or recessed lights. This type of light works well for television viewing, conversing with friends and family members, or simply relaxing on the sofa.

One of the easiest ways to increase overhead lighting is to upgrade an overhead fixture, a task the *Design on a Dime* design coordinators do regularly. If your room is already wired for a central fixture, consider replacing it with a chandelier. These attractive fixtures can serve as a lighting workhorse in almost any room in the house, from the kitchen and dining area to the bedroom, office, and even the bath. The key to choosing the perfect chandelier is to make sure the style of the fixture matches the style and the size of the room. A fixture that is too large can look overpowering and quite possibly produce light that's too harsh. A fixture that is too small can appear diminutive and may not adequately illuminate the entire room. For advice choosing the perfect chandelier, see "Chandelier Sizing" *above right.*

This dining room *opposite* glows with candlelight and exudes romance during the evening hours. To see more of it, turn to pages 168–175.

Chandelier Sizing

An easy way to determine the proper size of a chandelier is to measure the length and the width of the room and add the two numbers. The sum should be the diameter of the chandelier. For example, an 11×12-foot den requires a chandelier that is approximately 23 inches in diameter, while a 14×14-foot room needs a fixture that is about 28 inches across.

This college student's bedroom doubles as a homework center. See pages 176–181.

The Right Light for the Task

Follow these guidelines when choosing task lighting fixtures.

• To light a dressing table, add a table lamp fitted with a light, translucent shade at each side of the mirror, keeping the light source at about eye level. To maximize the lamp's reflective qualities, choose a light surface for the dressing tabletop.

• For comfortable reading in bed, position the bottom of the a lampshade about 20 inches above the top of the mattress.

• For desk work, such as paying bills, copying recipes, and writing letters, position the bottom of the lampshade at about eye level. The light output should be large enough to illuminate all your necessary papers and books.

• To read from a seated position, place a floor lamp above and over the shoulder. Short floor lamps, 40 to 42 inches high, should line up with your shoulder when you are seated. Taller lamps should be set about 15 inches to the side and 20 inches behind the center of the reading material. Check that the lamplight fully illuminates the reading surface without shadows or glare.

Task Lighting

As the name implies, this light illuminates a specific work or grooming area. Reading, sewing, cooking, shaving, and studying all require task lighting. You can create hardworking task lighting with well-placed table and floor lamps, downlights, and—in the kitchen and office—with undercabinet fixtures.

To generate task lighting, choose a fixture with a shade that focuses light in one area. If the shade is open at the top as well as the bottom, it can also supplement overall lighting. For reading and writing, the diameter of the beam spread out of the bottom of the shade should be at least 16 inches.

The type of shade you choose and the light output (lumens) of the bulbs used determine how much light a lamp produces. If you experience glare, the light output may be too high; if headaches or eyestrain occur, the light may be too dim. To save energy costs, find bulbs with the light output you need, and then choose the one with the lowest wattage. To reduce the possibility of an electrical fire, never exceed the lamp manufacturer's wattage maximum.

"Color affects light. A wall painted with flat white paint reflects 70 percent of the light that hits it. A black granite countertop or floor reflects only 10 percent of the light that hits it."
— Lee Snijders

Black and brown calm the vibrant
colors in this bedroom. See pages
176–181 for more on this space.

Mood-Enhancing Dimmer Switches
The ability to vary light levels can enhance the ambience of nearly any room. Dimmers are available in toggle, dial, or touch-sensitive styles. Before purchasing a dimmer switch, check to be sure it will work with your hardwired fixture. Unless equipped with a special dimmer, most fluorescents cannot be dimmed. Some halogen lights also require special dimmer switches.

Decorative lamps and light fixtures do more than shed light on a room; they also make a style statement. This hanging fixture, for example, declares that a fun and funky attitude rules the room.

Accent Lighting

This light provides the extra touch that makes a room sparkle. Illuminating a family portrait or a vase of flowers with a track light or a wall sconce, adding a tiny lamp to a bookshelf, or placing softly glowing candles around a bathtub are all examples of accent lighting. Accent lighting can also enhance architectural amenities and disguise problem areas through highlights and shadows.

To draw attention to a specific item, such as artwork, place an accent light at a 30-degree angle from a vertical surface and focus its beam on the object. Approximately three times the room's normal light level is required to spotlight an object. Similarly, spotlighting objects opposite problem areas—such as a corner with exposed piping or an ill-placed support beam—draws attention away from what you don't like and toward what you do.

Shade Secrets
Keep the following strategies in mind when lighting your home.
• Lampshades spread more light if they have a pale interior or liner.
• As a general rule, a lampshade should be approximately two-thirds the height of the lamp base, deep enough so that a small portion of the neck (the fitting between the lamp and the socket) is visible. The socket should be hidden. The shade should be about 1 ½ times the width of the lamp base.
• Before purchasing any lamp, ask if you can see it switched on; this may help you determine if the look and light output will fit your needs.
• For comfort, place a table lamp so that the bottom of the shade is at about eye level. When the shade is higher, the glare from the bulb can cause eyestrain.
• For the best look, keep bases and shades in proportion to the table; if the lamp makes the table appear top heavy, choose a smaller lamp or a larger table.

LIGHTBULBS

Type	Description	Pros	Cons
Incandescent	This is the original filament-style lightbulb that has been around for decades. The color of the emitted light is warm and flattering, mimicking natural light. The light level is easily controlled by a variety of different wattages, but you should never chose incandescent bulbs that have a higher wattage rating than the fixture manufacturer recommends. Incandescent bulbs are available in decorative shapes (candle flame, downlight globe, or tubular) and in clear, soft white, and colored styles. They also come in special-use varieties, including long-life and antivibration models.	These bulbs are the least expensive to purchase and come in a variety of shapes, styles, and lumen outputs to match almost any lamp requirement.	The bulbs use more energy (watts) per lumen than other bulb types, so they cost more than halogen and fluorescent bulbs in terms of energy usage.
Fluorescent	Fluorescent bulbs are available in long tubes and ring shapes that fit only in fixtures specified for fluorescents. They are also available as screw-in bulbs that fit many lamps and ceiling fixtures. Compact models are designed for use in special fixtures geared for tight spaces, such as in undercabinet lamps, as they generate less heat and last longer than incandescent bulbs.	The white light emitted by fluorescent bulbs is more illuminating and revealing than incandescent bulbs. Although more expensive than incandscent bulbs, the tubes last longer and are more energy-efficient.	Flourescent light is harsher and can be harder on the eyes and is less flattering than the light from the other bulb types.
Halogen	Halogen bulbs boast a bright white light that intensifies the colors in a room. These bulbs are designed to be long lasting, but fingertip oils that contact the bulb upon installation can cut the duration of the bulb in half. To help the bulb last longer, wear sandwich bags over your hand whenever handling a new bulb.	Halogen prices have dropped considerably in recent years, but they are still pricey compared to incandescent bulbs.	These bulbs get much hotter than the other bulb types, so they require a greater clearance between adjacent materials to prevent scorching.

For a soothing ambience, choose a candle- or oil-powered lamp. The flickering light is perfect for special dinners, quiet conversations, and long good nights.

The owners requested mismatched seating, but Kristan cautions that you can take a good thing too far. When choosing chairs for your dining room, limit the variety to two or three styles, then unify them through paint finish or fabric colors.

BEFORE

DINING LIGHT

The right dining light enhances your decor and contributes to a welcoming atmosphere for entertaining.

Design Goal

The owners of this bare-bones dining room requested a room attractive enough for formal entertaining, yet casual enough for family dinners.

Bright Ideas

When you imagine the perfect dining light, does a chandelier come to mind? If so, it might be because chandeliers have been lighting dining tables for centuries. Today's fixtures are better than ever—you can get more lumen output (brighter light) for less energy, and you can control the lumens at a whim by simply attaching your fixture to a dimmer control. If you'll be using your dining room for other activities, such as homework or bill paying, you may want to consider adding table lamps or pendent lights to illuminate work surfaces that share the space.

Light Sources

Before the *Design on a Dime* makeover, the brass chandelier chosen for this dining room was too small for the room (see page 163 for how to determine proper chandelier size), so Kristan opted to change it out, choosing a larger, brushed nickel fixture to complement the new steel hardware and aluminum accessories the design team added to the room. To provide light suitable for evening reading—a request of the homeowners—Kristan added a floor lamp next to the newly built window seat.

Artistic Highlights

In addition to general and task lighting, you'll also want to include plenty of accent lighting in this entertaining space. Set off an interesting architectural feature, such as a tray or vaulted ceiling, with rope lights hidden behind wide crown molding or wall sconces that direct the light up toward the ceiling. Then show off a favorite

Six Steps to Design Success

1. Planning. A new window seat, new chairs, a new chandelier, and lots of accent lighting make this dining room memorable and inviting.
2. Color. Warm caramel color paint covers the walls and unifies the design.
3. Furnishings. A bench and two styles of dining chairs provide a variety of seating options.
4. Fabric. Creamy and caramel color fabrics in three patterns complement the new color scheme.
5. Artwork. A dramatic mirror-backed display, a variety of taper candles, and a vase of fresh flowers fill the room with energy and life.
6. **Lighting. A new chandelier, a floor lamp, a large bay window, and the candles light the room in style day and night.**

Each of these jar candles costs less than $5. Although jar sizes vary, the creamy white wax color creates unity. For safety, always burn candles within sight (never leave burning candles unattended). Keep adjacent items clear of the flames.

Details, Details

Low-smoke, drip-free, unscented beeswax candles *above* are more expensive than basic wax candles, but they burn much more cleanly.

These lilies *above right* were purchased from a local farmer's market. You can achieve a similar effect with silk or with any fresh, seasonal blossoms.

Kristan made these pillows *right* from fabric remnants that were left over from the dining chairs and bench.

An area rug anchors the new dining arrangement *opposite* and provides warmth and comfort underfoot. Using a tablecloth in an unexpected size adds design flair.

piece of framed art with a picture light, or light up a display shelf with a spotlight.

To create enticing accent lighting in this dining room, Kristan made a large mirror-backed display and then filled the display shelves with a variety of jar candles. The mirrors double the light output from the candles and make an interesting and artistic focal point. More candles flicker atop the refinished buffet.

Flexible Furnishings

To make your dining room as flexible as possible, choose a table that is as comfortable for two as it is for a crowd. This table has multiple leaves that can be removed or inserted to make the table intimate enough for two or spacious enough for 12. To make the seating equally accommodating, Kristan opted for two side chairs, two host chairs, and a cushioned bench. When entertaining a larger crowd, the homeowners can bring in chairs from adjoining rooms to provide additional seating.

Formal Fabrics

Three fabric patterns are used on the chairs and then repeated on the tablecloth and the window seat cushions. A tone-on-tone stripe, muted floral, and tone-on-tone check fabric harmonize with new solid velvet drapery panels and a tone-on-tone pattern area rug. To create a color-coordinated look like this in your dining room, choose fabrics that feature only subtle color shifts.

Warm Color

Colors used in surrounding areas of this home defined the palette for this room; the only difference is that the colors here are more saturated. Deep, rich colors are good choices for dining rooms because these colors create an instant sense of intimacy and warmth.

Project Costs
Lighting: $97
Paint and supplies: $39
Furniture: $398
Fabric and window treatments: $281
Artwork and accessories: $183
Total Cost: $998

Visual Connections

Varying shades of caramel color appear in each of the fabrics used in this room, creating an overall sense of cohesiveness.

For this space, Kristan was able to purchase chairs in pairs. Then she supplemented the chair seating with a bench upholstered in a complementary fabric.

Dave built this window seat *opposite* from a frame of 2×4s and a finish-grade plywood top and front. Decorative wood panels attached to the front add architectural interest and match paneling used elsewhere in the home.

Candlelight transforms an ordinary dining room into a magical retreat. The flickering light not only becomes a focal point but also draws the eye to objects it illuminates. When choosing candles for your dining area, shop for unscented, smoke-free, drip-free varieties. Although these candles are the most costly, they will not interfere with the aroma or taste of your food. You can find smoke-free, drip-free candles at finer candle and home furnishing stores and on the internet.

A large mirrored display reflects light and can make a small room feel brighter and bigger.

MAKE A MIRRORED DISPLAY

Create this light-reflecting display using precut mirror tiles, particleboard, and jar candles. For a video demonstration, visit HGTV.com/dod.

Step-By-Step

1. Paint the particleboard back and shelves brown or desired color; let dry. If necessary apply a second coat of paint.

2. From the 1×4 board, cut three 24-inch lengths for backing and wall mounts. Referring to photo A, trim the 1-inch edges of the boards at an angle. Attach two boards to the back of the particleboard about 18 inches from the top, spacing them to slide snugly over the third board. Bolt the third board to wall studs about 60 inches above the floor (or at the desired height).

3. Lay the backing board faceup and arrange the mirror tiles and painted shelves. Use a pencil to mark the exact locations of the mirror tiles and shelves.

4. Attach the shelves to the particleboard backing using L brackets and wood screws.

5. Attach metal spacers to the particleboard where mirrors will be placed (photo B). This ensures that the mirrors attached atop the L brackets won't protrude farther from the backing than those attached directly to the backing.

6. Attach the mirrors to the spacers with heavy-duty all-surface glue (photo C); let the glue dry according to the manufacturer's instructions.

7. Slide the backing mounts over the wall mount. Place candles on the shelves.

You Will Need

Brown or desired color paint

Household paintbrush

¾-inch particleboard for the backing (backing shown is cut to 53 inches × 40 inches)

¾-inch particleboard OR finish-grade wood cut into shelves OR ready-made shelves (shelves shown are 3 inches × 12 inches and cut from particleboard)

1×4 board

Precut 12-inch mirror tiles (display shown requires 12 squares)

Pencil

Metal spacers (4 for each mirror tile)

Metal L brackets (2 brackets per shelf)

Wood screws

Heavy-duty glue

Jar candles

"The price of candles varies as much as their design, so always compare prices before making your final purchasing decisions."
— Kristan Cunningham

Floor-to-ceiling draperies draw attention to the ceiling height and make the room appear more spacious. A white bedspread also helps to open up the room.

BEFORE

COMFORT GLOW

In a multipurpose room, such as a combination bedroom and office, the lighting needs to be suitable for a variety of activities, from computer and paperwork to relaxation and rest.

Design Goal

Originally designed for a young teen, this small bedroom now needs to serve as a tranquil retreat and as a hardworking office for a full-time college student.

Before its *Design on a Dime* makeover, this tiny bedroom had only one small desk lamp and a tiny work surface. To study, the resourceful college student grabbed a floor lamp from the adjacent living room and pulled it next to the bed. If your bedroom or office lighting plan requires similar tactics, consider this: Appropriate lighting increases productivity, accuracy, and comfort and reduces eyestrain and fatigue.

Illuminating Tactics

For paperwork and computer work you'll need both overhead (ambient) lighting and localized (task) lighting. Ceiling lights and hanging fixtures are excellent sources of ambient lighting. Floor lamps like the one *opposite* can be used as a source of ambient light (especially when fitted with a three-way bulb that can match light output to your individual needs) or as a task light when focused on a specific area.

To create a shadow-free work surface, choose fixtures that are bright enough to illuminate the work area, but not so bright that they cause glare. Lamps with white shades (which reflect light without absorbing it) and light-color hanging fixtures are excellent sources for surface lighting, as are table lamps and recessed spots.

To light the work area in this bedroom, the team purchased low-voltage undercabinet halogen spotlights. These small, round fixtures are secured to the underside of the shelves with screws.

When your office work is done, you'll want task lighting focused on the head of the bed (as is the floor lamp *opposite*) and any bedroom grooming areas, such as a makeup vanity. To soften the

Six Steps to Design Success

1. Planning. Adding study space to this small bedroom was a priority.
2. Color. To prevent the space from feeling even smaller, the walls were painted a pastel shade, and a white comforter covers the bed.
3. Furnishings. A compact study area provides space for a computer and lots of books.
4. Fabric. Solid color fabrics lend an air of sophistication and prevent the room from looking too busy. Only the headboard boasts a large print.
5. Artwork and accessories. Mirrored silhouettes above the windows serve as interesting and reflective wall art. A few simple vases add design dash.
6. **Lighting. Halogen spots, a shell chandelier, and a versatile desk lamp supplement sunlight.**

Because this bedroom is small, to maximize floor space Dave attached these custom storage shelves to the wall.

Light Sources

A capezio shell chandelier *above* was purchased for under $30 and provides flickering accent light when the student is just hanging out with friends.

The floor lamp *above right* provides reading light when necessary or it can be turned upward to create ambient light.

These below-cabinet fixtures *right* are available from most lighting supply stores and attach to cabinet bottoms with just a few screws.

mood in the room, consider installing wall sconces to illuminate artwork or accessories. Uplights also create interesting contrasts between shadows and light.

Color and Fabric Reflections

The colors that you choose for your bedroom/office or combination space also affect the amount of lighting needed. A room decorated with dark colors—walnut paneling and navy carpet and furnishings, for example—will need two to three times more lamplight than an office decorated in whites and pastels. For the work surface itself, choose a matte finish. A shiny desktop made from high-gloss stone, wood, or laminate can contribute to glare and eyestrain.

For this double-duty bedroom, the design team chose pale lavender paint for the walls and kept the creamy beige wall-to-wall carpeting. A colorful headboard made from a contemporary shower curtain fabric and lively toss pillows contrast with an all-white comforter. A plum bedskirt and draperies and a lime green area rug pump up the accent color without making the room look too dark. The draperies hang from the ceiling to the floor to draw the eye up and increase the room's perceived volume. The desk area features walnut shelving and a white file cabinet and chair.

Accessory Shine

Mirrored wall art reflects light from the room's multiple lighting sources, as well as the sunlight that filters in from the three windows. A few well-placed china vases commingle with college textbooks to prevent the storage areas from looking too text-heavy. The end result is a hardworking, well-lit space that comfortably accommodates studying, relaxing, and even entertaining a few friends.

Project Costs
Bed area: $287
Work space: $260
Paint and mirrored wall art: $56
Window treatments: $253
Rug, chandelier, hardware, and
   accessories: $144
Total Cost: $1,000

A two-drawer filing cabinet doubles as desk base. A thrift store chair provides seating. For advice on covering a chair cushion like this one, see page 41.

MAKE A MIRROR-BACKED SILHOUETTE

If you like unusual wall art, you will love these silhouettes. You can make them in a few hours for less than $10 each.

Step-By-Step:

1. Cover each mirror with contact paper.

2. Use a pencil or pen to sketch or trace a silhouette onto the contact paper (photo A).

3. With a crafts knife, cut out the silhouette and then remove the cutout "head" (photo B).

4. Spray-paint the cutout area following the manufacturer's instructions (photo C). Let the paint dry thoroughly.

5. Carefully pull away the remaining contact paper (photo D). Hang the mirror tile as desired.

> **"Use mirrors as a canvas to make fun and affordable wall art for any room in your home."**
> – Spencer Anderson

You Will Need for Each

One 12-inch square mirror tile

Contact paper

Pencil or pen

Crafts knife

Spray paint

A

B

C

D

GLOSSARY

All-weather fabric: Mildew- and fade-resistant fabric designed for outdoor use.

Accent light: Lighting designed to enhance architectural amenities or display areas.

Accent table: Small side table that holds decorative accessories and/or a table lamp.

Adaptations: Furnishings that capture the flavor of the original but are not authentic.

Ambient light: General, overhead lighting that illluminates an entire room.

Analogous colors: Any series of colors that are adjacent on the color wheel.

Antique: Any object 100 or more years old.

Antiquing: A technique for applying paint, varnish, or glaze to a surface, then partially removing it to suggest age.

Architectural salvage: Any remnants of a dismantled building salvaged for use in another building or for display.

Armoire: A tall, freestanding wooden storage cabinet originally devised by the French in the 17th century to store armor.

Art Deco: A style of architecture and furnishings popular in the 1920s and 1930s; characteristics include streamlined shapes and geometric motifs and extensive use of glass, plastic, and chrome.

Art stand: A narrow table or pedestal used for displaying three-dimensional artwork.

Baker's rack: A decorative metal or wooden freestanding rack with multiple shelves.

Balance: A state of equilibrium, can be symmetrical or asymmetrical

Batting: Sheets or layers of raw cotton, wool, or a synthetic fibrous material used for lining quilts or stuffing upholstery or pillows.

Bay window: A projecting roofed structure that includes windows set at an angle to each other.

Buffet table: A narrow table often used in a dining room for serving dishes.

Cane: Rattan reeds created for use in wicker and basket weaving.

Canvas: A tightly woven cloth usually made from cotton or linen.

Case goods: Furniture industry terms for chests and cabinets.

Chair rail: A molding, usually of wood, running along a wall at the height of chair backs.

Chaise longue: An elongated chair designed for reading and relaxing

Chintz: Printed cotton, often glazed

Chroma: A hue's brightness or dullness.

Color washing: A painting technique that produces a finish ranging from subtle clouding to an underwater look.

Complementary colors: Colors that are opposite each other on the color wheel.

Computer armoire: A wooden cupboard specifically designed to hold a computer and printer.

Console: A rectangular table usually set against a wall in a foyer or dining room; also refers to a bracketed shelf attached to a wall.

Cornice: Horizontal molding at the top of a wall; also refers to a boxlike structure mounted above a window to conceal drapery hardware.

Credenza: A sideboard or buffet.

Decorator fabrics: Sold in 54-inch widths, these fabrics are made specifically for interior design. You'll need less yardage with these fabrics than you will with 45-inch-wide garment fabrics.

Downlight: Recessed or attached to the ceiling, a spotlight that casts light downward.

Drop-leaf table: A table with hinged leaves that can be folded down.

Eclectic: A style in which furnishings and accessories of various periods and styles are deftly and harmoniously combined.

Faux: French for "false," a term to describe something that is simulated.

Garment fabrics: Sold in 45-inch widths, these fabrics are made for the purpose of garment construction.

Gilding: A technique for applying gold to furniture and other surfaces.

Gold leaf: Wafer-thin sheets of gold used in gilding decorative objects.

Graining: A decorative paint technique that simulates the look of wood grain.

Grommet: Fastening rings similar to eyelets that reinforce holes in fabric.

Halogen: A type of light that uses metal halides in compact, highly efficient bulbs, tubes, and reflectors.

Hook-and-loop tape: A two-part fabric tape that fastens together by connecting a nubby "hooking" fabric to a looped fabric. Velcro® is a brand of hook-and-loop tape.

Hue: Another word for color.

Hutch: A two-part case piece that usually has a closed storage on the bottom and open shelves on the top.

Incandescent light: The kind of light that emanates from standard lightbulbs.

Indirect light: Light directed toward, then reflected from, a surface such as a wall or ceiling.

Miter box: A tool used to make perfectly diagonal cuts in wood.

Moiré: Fabric, usually silk, with a rippled, wavy pattern that gives a watered appearance.

Monochromatic colors: A color scheme limited to one color in various tones.

Patina: The natural finish on a wood surface that results from age and polishing.

Picture light: A shaded metal light fixture that projects over a picture to illuminate it.

Picture rail: A molding placed high on a wall as a means for suspending artwork.

Primary colors: Red, blue, and yellow, from which all other colors are derived.

Ragging: A textured effect produced by passing a crumpled rag over wet paint or glaze.

Reproduction: An exact, or nearly exact, copy of an original design.

Roman shade: A flat fabric shade that folds into neat horizontal pleats when raised.

Rope light: A string of small lightbulbs encased in a plastic sleeve.

Sari fabric: A fabric specifically made for the construction of women's wraparound dresses typically worn in southern Asia.

Scale: A term referring to the size of objects in relation to each other.

Secondary colors: Colors produced by mixing two primary colors; green, for example, is formed by mixing yellow and blue.

Silver leaf: Wafer-thin sheets of silver used in gilding decorative objects.

Sponging: A paint technique involving dabbing on colors with a sponge.

Studio apartment: A one-room (plus a bath) apartment.

Task light: Lighting that illuminated a specific work or grooming area.

Tertiary colors: Mixing a primary color with the secondary color next to it creates a tertiary color, such as orange-red or blue-green.

Tint: The lighter values of a particular color obtained by mixing the color with white.

Tone: The darkness or lightness of a color; different colors may be of the same tone.

Trompe l'oeil: French for "fool the eye"; a two-dimensional painting designed to look three-dimensional.

Uplight: A light fixture that directs light toward the ceiling.

Valance: A drapery treatment made of fabric or wood used as a heading.

Veneer: A thin layer of wood, usually of fine quality, that is bonded to a heavier surface of lesser quality wood. Most new furniture is made of veneer construction.

Wainscoting: Wood paneling applied to walls from baseboards to the desired height.

CREDITS AND RESOURCES

Pages 24–29 Episode 1113 Design Team: Kristan Cunningham, Spencer Anderson, Dave Sheinkopf. Photographer: T. Miyasaki Photographic Illustration. Resources: Anawalt Lumber; 818-769-4421. Behr Paint; available at Home Depot; 800-854-0133, ext. 2; www.behr.com. Jo-Ann Fabrics & Crafts; 888-739-4120; www.joann.com. Linens 'n Things; 866-568-7378, option 1; www.lnt.com. Burlington Coat Factory; 800-444-2628; www.Burlingtoncoatfactory.com. Marshalls; 888-627-7425; www.marshallsonline.com. Libby's Home and Garden; 323-663-2600. Joseph's Rugs; 7750 Balboa Blvd., Van Nuys, CA 91406.

Pages 30–35 Episode 1101 Design Team: Kristan Cunningham, Spencer Anderson, Dave Sheinkopf. Photographer: T. Miyasaki Photographic Illustration. Resources: Fabrics & Fabrics; 403 E 9th St.; Los Angeles, CA 90015. Journal Fabric; 213-624-0524. Home Fabrics; 213-689-9600. Target Department Store; 800-800-8800; www.target.com. IKEA North America; 800-434-4532; www.ikea.com. Pier 1 Imports; 800-245-4595; www.pier1.com. Behr Paint; available at Home Depot; 800-854-0133, ext. 2; www.behr.com. Mainly Seconds; 818-985-4499. Out of the Closet; 323-467-6811; www.aidshealth.com.

Pages 36–41 Episode 1105 Design Team: Kristan Cunningham, Spencer Anderson, Dave Sheinkopf. Photographer: Michael Garland. Resources: HomeGoods; 800-614-4663; www.homegoods.com. Rejuvenation; 888-401-1900; www.rejuvenation.com. Anna's Linens; 866-266-2728; www.annaslinens.com. IKEA North America; 800-434-4532; www.ikea.com. Behr Paint; available at Home Depot; 800-854-0133, ext. 2; www.behr.com. Liz's Antique Hardware; 323-939-4403; www.lahardware.com. Aaron Brothers Inc.; 888-372-6464; www.aaronbros.com.

Pages 42–47 Episode 1202 Design Team: Kristan Cunningham, Spencer Anderson, Dave Sheinkopf. Photographer: Michael Garland. Resources: Target Department Store; 800-800-8800; www.target.com. Linens 'n Things; 866-568-7378, option 1; www.lnt.com. The Great Indoors; 888-511-1155; www.thegreatindoors.com. HomeGoods; 800-614-4663; www.homegoods.com. Michaels; 800-642-4235; www.michaels.com. Jo-Ann Fabrics & Crafts; 888-739-4120; www.joann.com.

Pages 56–61 Episode 710 Design Team: Lee Snijders, Summer Baltzer, Charles Burbridge. Photographer: Michael Garland. Resources: Benjamin Moore Paints; www.benjaminmoore.com. Krylon; 800-457-9566; www.krylon.com. Joseph's Rugs, 818-679-8209; www.josephsrugs.com .

Pages 62–69 Episode 1109 Design Team: Kristan Cunningham, Spencer Anderson, Dave Sheinkopf. Photographer: Michael Garland. Resources: Cost Plus World Market; www.worldmarket.com. Bombay Kids; www.bombaykids.com. Behr Paint; available at Home Depot; 800-854-0133, ext. 2; www.behr.com. IKEA North America; 800-434-4532; www.ikea.com. Jo-Ann Fabrics & Crafts; 888-739-4120; www.joann.com.

Pages 70–75 Episode 1004 Design Team: Lee Snijders, Summer Baltzer, Charles Burbridge. Photographer: Michael Garland. Resources: Lowe's Companies, Inc.; 800-445-6937; www.lowes.com. Linens 'n Things; 866-568-7378, option 1; www.lnt.com. Canadian Art Prints; 800-663-1166; www.canadianartprints.com. Target Department Store; 800-800-8800; www.target.com. Benjamin Moore Paints; www.benjaminmoore.com. Mann Brothers; 888-618-6266; www.mannbrothers.com. California Tile; 818-846-5938.

CREDITS AND RESOURCES

Pages 84–89 Episode 1108 Design Team: Lee Snijders, Summer Baltzer, Charles Burbridge. Photographer: T. Miyasaki Photographic Illustration. Resources: Benjamin Moore Paints; www.benjaminmoore.com. Casa Victoria; 323-644-5590. Cost Plus World Market; www.worldmarket.com. Target Department Store; 800-800-8800; www.target.com. Macy's; www.macys.com. Wal-Mart; www.walmart.com. HomeGoods; 800-614-4663; www.homegoods.com. IKEA North America; 800-434-4532; www.ikea.com. Jo-Ann Fabrics & Crafts; 888-739-4120; www.joann.com. : Lowe's Companies, Inc.; 800-445-6937; www.lowes.com.

Pages 90–95 Episode 306 Design Team: Lee Snijders, Summer Baltzer, Charles Burbridge. Photographer: Michael Garland. Resources: Benjamin Moore Paints; 888-236-6667; www.benjaminmoore.com. Wertz Brothers Furniture; 310-477-4251; www.wertzbrothers.com. T.J. Maxx; 800-926-6299; www.tjx.com. Aaron Brothers Inc.; 888-372-6464; www.aaronbros.com. Superior Moulding; 818-376-1415. Office Depot; 888-463-3768; www.officedepot.com. Target Department Store; 800-800-8800; www.target.com.

Pages 96–103 Episode 1110 Design Team: Lee Snijders, Summer Baltzer, Charles Burbridge. Photographer: Michael Garland. Resources: Target Department Store; 800-800-8800; www.target.com. Macy's; www.macys.com. Wal-Mart; www.walmart.com. : Cost Plus World Market; www.worldmarket.com. HomeGoods; 800-614-4663; www.homegoods.com. IKEA North America; 800-434-4532; www.ikea.com.

Pages 112–119 Episode 1102 Design Team: Lee Snijders, Summer Baltzer, Charles Burbridge. Photographer: Michael Garland. Resources: Benjamin Moore Paints; www.benjaminmoore.com. Mark's Paint Store; 818-766-3949; www.markspaint.com. Jo-Ann Fabrics & Crafts; 888-739-4120; www.joann.com. IKEA North America; 800-434-4532; www.ikea.com. Jackalope West (Hollywood); 818-761-4022; www.jackalope.com. Lowe's Companies, Inc.; 800-445-6937; www.lowes.com.

Pages 120–125 Episode 1104 Design Team: Lee Snijders, Summer Baltzer, Charles Burbridge. Photographer: Michael Garland. Resources: Kmart Corporation; 866-562-7848; www.bluelight.com. Cottage Art; 562-924-6268; www.cottageart.com. Ace Hardware; www.acehardware.com. Jackalope West (Hollywood); 818-761-4022; www.jackalope.com.

Pages 126–131 Episode 1010 Design Team: Kristan Cunningham, Spencer Anderson, Dave Sheinkopf. Photographer: Michael Garland. Resources: Michaels; 800-642-4235; www.michaels.com. Linens 'n Things; 866-568-7378, option 1; www.lnt.com. HomeGoods; 800-614-4663; www.homegoods.com. Target Department Store; 800-800-8800; www.target.com. Behr Paint; available at Home Depot; 800-854-0133, ext. 2; www.behr.com. Hotel Surplus Outlet; 323-780-7474; www.hotelsurplus.com. Jo-Ann Fabrics & Crafts; 888-739-4120; www.joann.com.

Pages 140–147 Episode 1111 Design Team: Kristan Cunningham, Spencer Anderson, Dave Sheinkopf. Photographer: Michael Garland. Resources: Joseph's Rugs; 7750 Balboa Blvd., Van Nuys, CA 91406. Z Gallerie; 800-358-8288; www.zgallerie.com. Target Department Store; 800-800-8800; www.target.com. Eco Fabrics; 213-891-1522. The Great Indoors; 888-511-1155; www.thegreatindoors.com. The Home Depot U.S.A.

Inc.; 770-433-8211; www.homedepot.com. Kmart Corporation: 866-562-7848; www.bluelight.com. HomeGoods; 800-614-4663; www.homegoods.com. Marshalls; 888-627-7425; www.marshallsonline.com. Ross Stores; 800-945-7677; www.rossstores.com.

Pages 148–153 Episode 1009 Design Team: Lee Snijders, Summer Baltzer, Charles Burbridge. Photographer: T. Miyasaki Photographic Illustration. Resources: Benjamin Moore Paints; www.benjaminmoore.com. Target Department Store; 800-800-8800; www.target.com. Jo-Ann Fabrics & Crafts; 888-739-4120; www.joann.com. Ross Stores; 800-945-7677; www.rossstores.com.

Pages 154–159 Episode 1106 Design Team: Lee Snijders, Summer Baltzer, Charles Burbridge. Photographer: T. Miyasaki Photographic Illustration. Resources: Benjamin Moore Paints; www.benjaminmoore.com. IKEA North America; 800-434-4532; www.ikea.com. Costco; www.costco.com. Wallpapers To Go; 800-843-7094; www.wallpaperstogo.com. California Tile Distributors, Inc.; 818-846-5938.

Pages 168–175 Episode 611 Design Team: Kristan Cunningham, Spencer Anderson, Dave Sheinkopf. Photographer: Michael Garland. Resources: Hotel Surplus Outlet; 323-780-7474; www.hotelsurplus.com. Al's Discount Furniture; 818-255-4740; www.alsdiscountfurniture.com. The Great Indoors; 888-511-1155; www.thegreatindoors.com. Michael Levine; 213-239-0909; www.mlfabrics.com. The Home Depot U.S.A. Inc.; 770-433-8211; www.homedepot.com. Kmart Corporation: 866-562-7848; www.bluelight.com. Industrial Metal Supplies; 818-729-3333; www.imsmetals.com. General Wax &

Candle Company; 800-929-7867; www.genwax.com. IKEA North America; 800-434-4532; www.ikea.com. Behr Paint; available at Home Depot; 800-854-0133, ext. 2; www.behr.com.

Pages 176–181 Episode 1107 Design Team: Kristan Cunningham, Spencer Anderson, Dave Sheinkopf. Photographer: T. Miyasaki Photographic Illustration. Resources: Urban Outfitters; 800-282-2200; www.urbanoutfitters.com. IKEA North America; 800-434-4532; www.ikea.com. Jo-Ann Fabrics & Crafts; 888-739-4120; www.joann.com. Behr Paint; available at Home Depot; 800-854-0133, ext. 2; www.behr.com. Linens 'n Things; 866-568-7378, option 1; www.lnt.com. Al Greenwood; 562-498-9277.

INDEX

INDEX

to some, inspiration comes naturally.
for the rest of us, may we suggest a good book?

Make that three good books. In all three, you'll find simple and affordable design ideas, not to mention plenty of inspiration. For more great *Design on a Dime* ideas, watch the new team, designer Brice Cooper and design coordinators Kelly Edwards and Ali, as they transform ordinary rooms into awesome spaces.

YOU SHOULD SEE WHAT'S ON

HGTV.com